# Two Trees Series

First published in 2020 by Dick Bell MBE

# The Holy Spirit
## by Dick Bell MBE

The Holy Spirit

# Contents

# Prologue: The Holy Spirit.

So few understand the Holy Spirit. That is because He is so gentle, so humble, and so self-effacing. He hides. Particularly, He hides behind Jesus. If there is any promotion of Jesus anywhere in the world, it is the Holy Spirit who has generated it – whatever other channels it may have come through. No one knows Him, unless He reveals Himself to them. And He never does that until we repent of all our self-stupidities and ask Jesus to forgive us.

But, like the wind, you cannot grab Him. You can see what He is doing, or what He has done, but not Him doing it. Mind you, He leaves a trail behind Him, a bit like a snail does. There is no mistaking the thrill, the joy, the overwhelming surprise that opens up our minds - when He comes. He brings fresh air, fresh cleansing, fresh inspiration with Him. He pushes Jesus to the forefront, and He leaves Jesus behind when He has gone.

The Holy Spirit is a very special gift, coming special delivery, from Jesus, to mark what He did on this earth. Jesus was so successful, and so complete with what He did in his 33 years on earth, that God the Father asked Him what He would like as a present. His answer was to send the Holy Spirit down to all mankind (John 16:7). So now, God the Trinity is living inside every human being – a very special and new arrangement once Jesus had returned home to heaven. But God is so gentle, so humble, and hides. You don't know He is in there, unless you ask. He talks to us from inside out, but we do not know it is Him (some call Him conscience). That is, until we receive Jesus into our hearts as Lord and Saviour. That is when we really feel the Holy Spirit and know His presence on our insides, because He opens our eyes to heaven, and He gives us a new birth into a new life and a new dimension.

Interestingly, He does not change His pattern. He still talks to us inside, still so quietly, still so gently, but now, when we have been born from above by the Holy Spirit and become a Christian, we have the connection of faith to make all our communications real and personal. From then on, all our days should be filled with joy and gladness, for Jesus has redeemed us from all our stupidities, and the Holy Spirit is constantly nudging us with Divine acceptance.

Read all about it in this booklet. God loves you; Jesus has rescued you; you are a King or Queen in His Kingdom; and the Holy Spirit will give you an equivalent of "Yippee" inside you every day (if you let Him).

# Our Lovely Holy Spirit.

Gentle. Quiet. Humble. Self-effacing. Kind. Promotional of others. Forgiving. Friend. Fun, but ever controlled. Servant. Good. Gracious. Never condemnatory.

Please add to those characteristics of the Holy Spirit out from your own riches in Jesus Christ.

Who can describe such a humble Being? Who can exalt Someone who never wants to be exalted? Who can make King Someone who never wants to be King, but is eternally content to be the humble servant of The King? We try to raise Him up because of the beautiful things He does to us and in us, but He slides away and demotes Himself again and again. How can we exalt a friend in whom there is no self?

In this little booklet I have analysed some characteristics of the Holy Spirit. That analysis seems harsh in the light of His gentle heart. He softens everything He touches. He makes beautiful every genuine song of worship to Jesus, every conversation that promotes Jesus, every little action that is done in Jesus' name. He rounds off every sharp-edged corner. Quietly and so silently He births Jesus into the hearts of penitent human beings, never declaring that it is He who has done it. Like the wind, you cannot see Him, do not know where He is from or where He is going, such is God's precious Holy Spirit. But you certainly know His effect!

He is the arch communicator of the heart and soul of God the Father. God's eternal love and unfathomable grace is brought to bear, so wisely, so sweetly and so imperceptibly to apply exactly where it is needed in the second it is needed in the souls of human beings. God *loves* people. He really does. That love is enshrined in careful wisdom – never too much and never too little – and brought to bear by the touch of His Holy Spirit.

Jesus did a lovely thing for the Holy Spirit. I think He did that because the Holy Spirit was His dearest, most intimate and gentlest Friend. He said, *"And so I tell you, every kind of sin and slander can be forgiven, but blasphemy against the Spirit will not be forgiven. Anyone who speaks a word against the Son of Man will be forgiven, but anyone who speaks against the Holy Spirit will not be forgiven, either in this age or in the age to come."* (Matt 12:31-32). The Holy Spirit is mega-sensitive. Paul said *"And do not grieve the Holy Spirit of God, with whom you were sealed for the day of redemption."* (Eph 4:30). He is able to be grieved. If we grieve Him, He runs away fast. His gentleness can be hurt.

How complete are the Trinity! Father God who is immense above all, Jesus the Son who is the hands-on terminator of sin and transmitter of salvation, and the lovely Holy Spirit who is the applicator of all God's healing medicine to wounded men and women. Indescribable, unfathomable, eternal, uncontainable, but lovely in the extreme. Such a God is worth dying for.

I beg you, cultivate your every moment of friendship with God's ever-present Holy Spirit. Love and serve the Servant of the Most High God.

The Holy Spirit

# The Holy Spirit.

The Holy Spirit is a He, not an It. Everyone without Revelation from God will have their own calculation as to who they think the Holy Spirit is, and, without Biblical knowledge and revelation, they will invariably get Him wrong. Indeed, I think that, unless we know Him personally, we will always have to rely on our own thinking for our understanding, and that will always be in error. The Bible will show this later.

He is one of the Godhead. He is just as much God as the Father and the Son. They are indivisible. The Trinity is One, and nothing will divide or separate them. The Holy Spirit is a Person, and I will show you many personal attributes that characterise His personal nature.

But first let us go back and see the Biblical history. The Holy Spirit has been around from the beginning of time, hovering over the waters in the creation, and empowering people in the Old Testament to do marvellous things. But things changed after Jesus died.

The cross of Jesus was so complete in its redemption, so perfect in its sacrifice, so entire in its cleansing from all sin that Jesus was enabled to send the Holy Spirit down to earth in an unrestricted way with redemption availability. Jesus neutralised all sin and death. Before Jesus came, the Holy Spirit was limited in His work. After Jesus died and rose again, the Holy Spirit can now indwell every person who is "in Christ" without any restriction or restraint. Sin is no longer a barrier.

Jesus said that it would be better that He left the earth and that He sent the Holy Spirit down to replace Him (John 16:7). Why? Because Jesus was limited in His geography (only one place at one time). But the Holy Spirit would not be boundaried by those limitations. He would be in all places at all times, thereby enabling the presence of God Himself to be available to every person throughout their lives, wherever they lived, in whatever century, and until the date when Jesus returns to rule on the earth.

I still find God's plan of Grace so complete and so perfect that it is perfect in every respect, and full of love and everything good and wholesome. What wisdom! What love! What grace!

And here I am writing this in the Epoch of Grace. That God should have worked Himself into a position that He need never condemn or judge anyone while they are living, but to reserve all assessments until everyone's lives are over is such a risky strategy that I marvel at it. He just keeps silent when we go our own way and reserves judgement until later, meanwhile sending His Holy Spirit to correct, redirect and gently steer us back into a way that blesses us and pleases Him. That's Grace. Magnificent, overwhelming Grace. One of the other things the Holy Spirit does is to boundary everyone's activities so that they never go beyond the reach of the grace of God. So the Hitlers, Stalins and Pol Pots of this world were boundaried in their genocides; none of them were allowed to go beyond God's grace. They were permitted to do what they did, but no more. We have to trust in the limits which God imposes on each human being.

## So, who is the Holy Spirit?

Jesus told Thomas (John 14) that He (Jesus) was exactly like His Father. "He who has seen me has seen the Father. Thomas, how come you never knew that, having lived with me for three years? I am exactly like my Dad. There are no differences between us." And then Jesus talked about the Holy Spirit whom He would send. *"I will ask the Father, and he will give you another Counsellor to be with you for ever – the Spirit of truth."* (John 14:16).

But I now have to go to the Greek. There are things that are not obvious at all in English, and the New Testament was deliberately written in Greek just so that we could have little gems made clear for us. So, the one English word "another" comes in two forms in Greek. *Allos* means "Another of the same kind", and *heteros* means "Another of a different kind." (We use the word *heteros* in English – heterosexual, heterodox, heterogeneous etc.) So, for example, heterosexual means "another" of the same kind of creature but of a different sex, like a male and female lion – same species, different gender. Now whenever the Bible uses "another" talking about the Holy Spirit, it is always *allos* – "another of the *same* kind".

What was Jesus saying? He was saying that the Holy Spirit was exactly like Himself, just as He was exactly like His Father. You cannot separate the Trinity, nor can you separate their characteristics. They are all perfect and complete and the same in every respect. The Biblical God that you know, you can call "Jesus", "Father" or "Holy Spirit". Take your pick. They are never offended, because you cannot get it wrong. What you say of one you say of all three. They are "another of the same kind". So you can never (and must never) split the Trinity.

What about the Holy Spirit's nature? An IT or a HE? Many get that wrong.

I have to return to the Greek again. The Greek word for "Spirit" (*pneuma*) is neuter. (By the way, it also means "wind" as in John 3:8 *"The wind blows wherever it pleases. You can hear its sound, but you cannot tell where it comes from or where it is going. So it is with everyone born of the Spirit."* Wind and Spirit in that passage are interchangeable). The gender of nouns is not important in English, but it is very important in Greek, and in many other Mediterranean languages. Why? Because adjectives and antecedents have to agree with the gender of the noun (masculine, feminine or neuter). Therefore, all adjectives or antecedents that refer to *pneuma* should be neuter. But now see John 16:11-14. *"But when he, the Spirit of truth comes, he will guide you into all truth. He will not speak on his own: he will speak only what he hears, and he will tell you what is to come. He will bring glory to me by taking from what is mine and making it known to you."* Let me remind you that the word *pneuma*, Spirit, is neuter. In this passage, correct Greek should read, "But when it, the Spirit of truth comes, it will guide you into all truth. It will not speak on its own: it will speak only what it hears, and it will tell you what is to come. It will bring glory to me by taking what is mine and making it known to you." But John has deliberately written bad Greek just to make sure no one gets it wrong, and makes the Holy Spirit a He, and definitely not an It. John always makes the Holy Spirit a Person, not a Thing. Everyone who knows Jesus personally also knows the Holy Spirit personally, as I show next.

## Being Born of the Spirit.

A Christian is someone who is born of the Spirit. In John 3 Jesus made this plain. Human beings (and all living things) are conceived by the fertilisation of egg by sperm. *Christians* are conceived into *God's* family by fertilisation of their human spirit by the Holy Spirit. The parallels are complete and perfect. Just as no human being can be conceived in any other way than by human fertilisation, so no one can become a Christian in any other way than by being "born of water and the Spirit" (John 3:5-6). *"Flesh gives birth to flesh, but the Spirit gives birth to spirit."* It is absolute. There is no other way for either to happen. It is the work of the Holy Spirit to make this happen. Therefore everyone conceived and born of the Holy Spirit knows Him personally. The opposite is also true – those who do not know the Holy Spirit personally have not yet been brought to birth by Him. You can tell – anyone who calls the Holy Spirit "It", is not born from God, and is *not* a Christian.

# Being Filled with the Holy Spirit.

When talking about the Holy Spirit's activity in mankind, the Bible makes it very clear that there is a distinction between "with", "in" and "on". The Holy Spirit is "with" everyone to bring them to Jesus. When a person is born of the Spirit, the Holy Spirit comes "in" (John 14:17). But every Christian to whom this has happened needs also to be filled with the Spirit. That is, the Holy Spirit needs to come "on" them, a parallel expression to "being filled".

In the Old Testament this is clear. Particularly in Judges, the Holy Spirit came "on" certain leaders to achieve the exploits they did. Othniel, Gideon, Jephthah, Samson, and David are examples.

So let me try to clear up some misunderstandings. To be "baptised" in the Spirit is the first occasion in which we are "filled" with the Spirit. Baptisms are always initiations. In the New Testament people were "filled" with the Spirit many times, and Christians today should also experience the same pattern. Paul urges *Be **being** filled with the Spirit."* (Eph 5:18) (a correct rendering of that scripture).

The Disciples were in a different position from those who have followed them throughout the centuries, because they lived both before and after Jesus' death and resurrection. So Jesus said to them while He was still alive, *"But you know him (i.e. the Holy Spirit), for he lives **with** you and will be **in** you."* (John 14:17). The Holy Spirit was "with" them, just as He is "with" all of us before we become Christians. He would then be "in" them when they actually became Christians. After Jesus had died and had risen from the dead, in one of His visits to the disciples, He said. *""Peace be with you! As the Father has sent me, I am sending you." And with that he breathed on them and said, "Receive the Holy Spirit.""* (John 20:21). I would think that this was the occasion when the disciples were born again of the Spirit – when the Holy Spirit came "in" them. Then, at Pentecost in Acts 2, the Holy Spirit came "on" them, and they were empowered to do mighty things for God. From then on, they were filled with the Spirit a number of times.

The records in Acts of the baptism and filling of the Holy Spirit indicate that God selected five particular incidents (Acts 2, 8, 9, 10, 19) from thousands to give us a full handle on what the Holy Spirit does and how. All indicate that Christians need both – to be born again of the Spirit and then to be filled with the Spirit for an effective life of power.

All the incidents of filling in Acts were accompanied by supernatural signs, none of which are consistent with each other. So, Biblically, there is not "one" sign of the filling of the Holy Spirit, but many. Some Churches teach that speaking in tongues is the sign of being filled with the Spirit (because it is the most common and easiest to do), but that is not consistent with all the New Testament illustrations. Paul, for instance, was cured from his blindness when he was filled with the Spirit, although he spoke in tongues later.

Acts 19 is particularly relevant. Paul was visiting Ephesus, and came across a small group of believers (about 12). He worshipped with them. But he was troubled. After the meeting was over, he asked, "Did you receive the Holy Spirit when you believed?" Why should he ask such a question? I think it's obvious – there were no signs of the Holy Spirit's presence – none of the gifts of 1 Cor 12. They replied, "Never heard of him. Who is he?"

So Paul asked another question. "What kind of baptism did you receive then?" Why should he ask *that* question? I think that's also obvious – all the other illustrations in Acts indicate that after water baptism of believers, the leaders immediately prayed for the Holy Spirit to come *on* those believers who had been baptised. Which He invariably did with supernatural signs. And clearly this was the normal pattern for people becoming Christians in those days – and should be as well today. So they replied, "John's baptism."

"Aha," said Paul. "John's baptism was one of repentance for the forgiveness of sins. Let me teach you about believer's baptism." So he taught them the New Testament pattern. They accepted it, believed in Jesus for the remission of their sins, were baptised again in water, Paul prayed for them to be filled with the Holy Spirit, and they all spoke in tongues and prophesied – clearly the signs that were originally missing. (As a matter of interest, this indicates that you can be baptised in water a second time if you got it wrong the first time). I think it is time the Christian Church returned to the Biblical pattern of Christian initiation.

Let me complete this aspect of the Holy Spirit by looking at the life of Jesus. We know He was conceived by the Holy Spirit. But there is no record of Him achieving anything exceptional for 30 years of His life until His water baptism by John the Baptist. There the Holy Spirit came "on" Him, and perhaps His "sign" was His Father's voice saying, *You are my Son, whom I love; with you I am well pleased.* (I suggest that maybe the "like a dove" sign was for John, not Jesus (see John 1:32-33)). From then on all sorts of exceptional things came from Him. Luke 4 is perhaps the best record of this, where His new life is described as "Full of the Holy Spirit", "was led by the Spirit", and "returned in the power of the Spirit". And the rest is history. So if there is any Christian reading this who thinks they do not need to be baptised and filled with the Holy Spirit, please think again. If Jesus, as a man, needed to be, who do we think we are that we don't? It seems to me that none of us will ever be the person God wants us to be until we are in possession of all the free gifts He says we need, and which He has graciously provided. (And, by the way, Water Baptism too!).

As Son of Man, Jesus *could* not do any miracles until He was baptised in the Holy Spirit – any more than we can.

Incidentally, there is no record of Jesus speaking in tongues. And I am so glad that He still does not speak in unknown languages to me – however much I may bombard Him with them.

The Holy Spirit

# The Holy Spirit's Task.

At Pentecost Jesus released the Holy Spirit on all mankind. Previously the Spirit had been restricted to individuals. But the cross has removed all barriers between man and God, so the Holy Spirit could now be free to indwell anyone on earth. He is a crucial part of God's invasion of earth.

There is a sequence that happened before God could release His Holy Spirit.

The first is that God the Father gave everything He has to Jesus, and has given Jesus all authority over everything, in heaven *and* on earth. Because Jesus was so faithful on earth, God has delegated the whole affairs of earth to Him. When Jesus has taken authority over all things and gained the victory over satan and all evil, He will hand the completed package back to God the Father (1 Cor 15:24-25), the last enemy being death.

The second is that the Holy Spirit can only give to us what Jesus has. John 16:14-15 tells us that. *"He will glorify me because it is from me that he will receive what he will make known to you. All that belongs to the Father is mine. That is why I said the Spirit will receive from me what he will make known to you."* Because God has delegated everything He has to Jesus, the Holy Spirit takes what Jesus has got and gives that to us.

The third thing is that Jesus has all authority over everything – as I have written. Therefore the Holy Spirit takes Jesus' authority, power and purpose, gleaned at a moment's notice, and makes that available to us at every moment in time. The Holy Spirit does nothing on His own. He is the messenger – or the Advocate, as Jesus described Him. Although He is God, He is so humble that He never uses any of His own power or authority in His dealings with us.

So I asked the Lord why He has arranged for it to work that way.

The answer was simple. Because Jesus lived a perfect human life on earth, and was tempted in *all* points like we are yet had no sin, He is the only human being in the universe who can counsel mankind on how to live without sin. All His suggestions are perfect. The course of action that He suggests is absolutely perfect. There is no more perfect thing that is possible to do in the whole universe than the thing that Jesus recommends. No one can get it better than that.

Therefore the Holy Spirit, who has never been a human being, takes Jesus suggestions and gives those to us.

That is His task in a nutshell.

The beauty of the cross is that, because of what it dealt with, the Holy Spirit can be released to all mankind to proclaim the rescue Jesus realised for us. No sin can separate any human being from the rescue God accomplished through Jesus.

Because the Holy Spirit is universal, the work of redemption (in humans, in business, in economy, in the environment, in everything) can now become perfect. All everyone has to do is to listen to the Holy Spirit's promptings and the whole world accomplishes God's will and would be perfect as the Kingdom of God on earth. Didn't Jesus suggest we pray "Your Kingdom come, your will be done on earth as it is in heaven"? The only way that that can be accomplished is to be perfect like Jesus was on earth, and we do that by listening to the Holy Spirit's suggestions and doing them.

The interesting thing is to see the enormity that Jesus left behind in heaven when He came to earth. His life on earth was strictly limited by God, so that He could simply accomplish the One Thing that God needed from Him in the totally appropriate way of doing it (to do God's will only by faith). It is the same for us. We all have One Major Task which the Lord has designated for our lives. In heaven, we will probably be much more able. But we first need to be proven faithful in the limited task on earth that the Lord has for us.

And we have an enemy.

Which is why we, living in the 21$^{st}$ century, are still living in a spoilt, degraded, wicked world. And why we are still in the battle that has been raging since Adam and Eve walked the earth.

Because God came down and rescued me, I am now part of an army that I previously knew nothing about. I have changed sides. So, whether I like it or not, I am fighting on God's side in a war I didn't choose to be in. I have an unavoidable part to play in bringing the goodness and glory of heaven to a dark world.

The great thing is that I have the mighty Victor by my side directing me; I have the Holy Spirit inside me giving me the Victor's directives, and I am guaranteed success. In addition, my life's plans and ambitions have been changed by this whole affair. No longer do I work for myself. No longer am I helping to "keep the world turning over into perpetuity". No longer am I flying aeroplanes and by it enjoying life to the full. Now I am simply single-mindedly helping Jesus to rescue the rest of mankind. And, from that, the cosmos (eventually).

The Holy Spirit's task is to enable me to do it.

# Characteristics of the Holy Spirit.

## The Personality of the Holy Spirit.

1 Corinthians 2 is, in my view, one of the most important and fruitful chapters in the whole Bible. It tells of how Paul was able to evangelise the vast city of Corinth in 18 months, of what wisdom is and where it comes from, of the stupidity and ignorance of satan and his demons, in superlatives of what awaits the Christian in the kingdom of heaven, and of the work of the Holy Spirit. So what does Paul say about the Holy Spirit?

1. **He brings Revelation.** *"No eye has seen, no ear has heard, no mind has conceived what God has prepared for those who love him – but God has revealed it to us by his Spirit." (9-10)* The Holy Spirit is God's method of conveying every kind of Revelation that comes to us in this epoch.

2. **He knows the Mind of God.** *"The Spirit searches all things, even the deep things of God...In the same way, no one knows the thoughts of God except the Spirit of God." (10-11)* I have written elsewhere and below that no one can understand God without divine revelation. This verse emphasises that truth – that no one knows who God is or what He thinks. Only the Holy Spirit can find that out. And only the Holy Spirit can reveal it to us. The Bible is absolutely consistent on this theme.

3. **He indwells the Christian.** *"We have not received the spirit of the world but the Spirit that is from God..."(12)* It is worth my pointing out that there is a spirit of worldliness, which far too many people have embraced. But it is in conflict with the Spirit that is from God. But the Spirit that is from God is exactly the opposite of worldliness. It is heavenly. He is gentle, but always consistent in His dealings with mankind.

4. **He Teaches Christians the Gifts and Grace of God.** *"..that we may understand what God has freely given us."(12)* Only the Holy Spirit knows the full extent of what God has done for us. What God has freely given us is so astonishing, so revolutionary, and so enormous that few Christians can grasp it, and fewer still believe it. Did you also notice that the Holy Spirit teaches? He is not only a counsellor, He is an instructor. He is also the Spirit of Truth (John 14:17).

5. **Christians should be Retelling what the Holy Spirit has first taught them.** *"This is what we speak, not in words taught us by human wisdom but in words taught by the Spirit, expressing spiritual truths in spiritual words."(13)* Things Christians say should be spiritual - that is, God-

honouring.. Our words should reflect the character and nature of God Himself – His love, compassion, care, kindness, grace, forgiveness and all the rest. The Holy Spirit teaches us the nature of God, and our speech then starts to reflect our walk with Him. The longer we walk with Him, the more Christ-like our speech becomes. Note that there is a human wisdom. But Christians should be speaking spiritual wisdom. Far too many speak a mixture of human and divine wisdom. When we do, are we surprised that our words become mediocre in their effect, lacking power and effectiveness? As we read our Bibles and the Holy Spirit opens them up to us, our hearts change. Then our speech changes, for *"Out of the overflow of the heart the mouth speaks."* (Luke 6:45). But there are occasions when we need words of knowledge and words of wisdom. These are gifts of the Holy Spirit given in the immediate as the need requires, and which we have no human way of knowing. (See 1 Cor 12:8). That makes Him a person. "Things" don't speak. But Christians should be utterly different from other human beings. Our lives, our attitudes, our words should bring life, happiness and joy to those we encounter. God is a happy God. So should we be too.

6.  **Spiritual Discernment.** *"The man without the Spirit does not accept the things that come from the Spirit of God, for they are foolishness to him, and he cannot understand them, because they are spiritually discerned."(14).* So who is this "man without the Spirit"? The Greek reads "The soul-centred man". That's not quite the same, although the principle is. The AV translates it "The natural man". We presume here that it is talking about a non-Christian. A normal man. Normal men are both soul-centred and without the Spirit. *Those* people, it very clearly says, are *absolutely incapable* of any spiritual discernment. The word "cannot" is absolute - no exceptions. Indeed, spiritual issues are utter folly to them. *Only* the Holy Spirit can bring heavenly understanding. This verse is so important to our understanding of the human condition and what it is not capable of.

7.  **Heavenly Insight.** *"The spiritual man makes judgments about all things, but he himself is not subject to any man's judgment: "For who has known the mind of the Lord that he may instruct him?" But we have the mind of Christ."(15-16).* The spiritual person exclusively has God's mind on all matters (provided they bother to listen). But take care – it says that *we* have the mind of Christ – not *I*. The mind of Christ is found collectively, not individually. And it is the Holy Spirit who brings the

mind of Christ to bear on all issues that confront the collective Church. Notice, too, that it is the individual who can make judgements on all things, but the *confirmation* must come *collectively*. It is our safeguard, and stops dominant Christian people from becoming control freaks.

8.  So what do these verses teach us about the Holy Spirit? He thinks. He discerns. He reads. He knows. He speaks. He conveys. All these actions are actions of a person and a personality. He is not an It!

## Holy Spirit Intercession.

*"In the same way, the Spirit helps us in our weakness. We do not know what we ought to pray for, but the Spirit himself intercedes for us with groans that words cannot express. And he who searches our hearts knows the mind of the Spirit, because the Spirit intercedes for the saints in accordance with God's will."* (Rom 8:25-27).

This teaches us a lot about intercession. Firstly, it is quite clear — we do not know how to pray or what to pray for. Only God knows His will in relation to prayer for others. Intercession is empathising with another person and weeping internally on their behalf. It is a cry of the heart. And it is based on the mind of God for that person — praying into their lives the will of God and the best possible for them (which only God knows). The Holy Spirit is the very best at it, and He groans and weeps the will of God for us inside. In addition, Jesus is also interceding for us (Heb 7:25, Rom 8:34).

The word "intercede" means "to go between". (The word "*pre*cede" means to go before. The word "*suc*ceed" means to go after. They come from the same root (actually Latin)). Jesus is the classic Intercessor. He stands between us and God, with one hand holding our hand, and the other holding God's hand, joining us together (and incidentally forming a cross in between). When we intercede for others, that is what we do: we hold Jesus' hand in one of ours, and the person for whom we are praying in the other, linking the two together. The cross that we form when we do that is an indicator of the sacrifice needed for intercession. That is also what the Holy Spirit does, with groans too deep to be expressed.

## Holy Spirit Conviction.

*"When he (the Holy Spirit) comes, he will convict the world of guilt in regard to*

*sin, righteousness and judgement.*" (John 16:8). No one but the Holy Spirit can convict the world of its sin. Many preachers try their hardest to make others feel guilty. Silly people. Have they never read their Bibles? If we preach what God is asking us to preach, regardless of our human perceptions, then the Holy Spirit will bring the mind of God to every listener. Those who need convicting will be convicted. Those who need encouraging will be encouraged. Those who need teaching will be taught. Those who need to relax will be given peace. I have pointed out elsewhere that a sermon is a miracle of grace. Everyone listening to God during it will be given appropriate revelation that is perfectly tuned to his or her situation. That is the work of the Spirit and is not able to be duplicated. No argument, no logic, no fiery emotion, *nothing* in the whole of creation can do what only the Holy Spirit can do.

## Teaching and Reminding.

*"But the Counsellor, the Holy Spirit, whom the Father will send in my name, will teach you all things and will remind you of everything I have said to you."* (John 14:26). The Holy Spirit will teach us all things. *He* will be our teacher. He will also be our memory. But that memory will be exclusive – He will remind us only of those things that Jesus communicates to us; which, incidentally, should be about all things every day of our lives. Again, these characteristics are not inanimate – they belong to a personality.

## Love.

*"And hope does not disappoint us, because God has poured out his love into our hearts by the Holy Spirit, whom he has given us."* (Rom 5:5). The Holy Spirit loves, and transmits God's love to us.

## Other Characteristics of the Holy Spirit.

*"For the kingdom of God is not a matter of eating and drinking, but of righteousness, peace and joy in the Holy Spirit,"* (Rom 14:17). Those good things are what characterises the Holy Spirit and also what He brings. He is the perfect representative of Jesus, who is the perfect representative of God the Father. The three have exactly the same characteristics, are all part of God, are all perfect, but have different roles. What an immense privilege it is for us to belong to such a beautiful and humble God.

## The Victory of the Holy Spirit.

*"So I say, live by the Spirit, and you will not gratify the desires of the sinful nature. For the sinful nature desires what is contrary to the Spirit, and the Spirit what is contrary to the sinful nature. They are in conflict with each other, so that you do not do what you want. But if you are led by the Spirit, you are not under law."* (Gal 5:16-18)

These verses tell us two brilliant things. First, they tell us that the Holy Spirit provides the power within us to overcome all the weaknesses and vulnerabilities of the flesh.

Secondly, they tell us that we can fulfil the law absolutely by "walking in the Spirit". Not by our own efforts or knowledge of the law at all – but by His power and grace (see Eph 2:8 onwards).

In other words, living by the Spirit is real freedom - practical, realistic and effective freedom from everything that would either tempt us or condemn us.

## The Power of the Holy Spirit.

*""Not by might nor by power, but by my Spirit," says the LORD Almighty."* (Zech 4:6). *"You will receive power when the Holy Spirit comes on you."* (Acts 1:8), All man's efforts to please God – and thereby to accomplish anything worthwhile on earth – are futile. The only way to please God is by His Spirit working in us and through us. Please remember – no one can duplicate the work of the Holy Spirit. If we want to do a work on earth that will last for ever (or for a very long time after we have died), then it has to have been initiated by the Holy Spirit, worked through by the Spirit, carried on by the Spirit, and completed by the Spirit. We are His servants, not His masters. And He invariably glorifies Jesus because all the power He has belongs first to Jesus.

Peter Morris said: "If you took the Holy Spirit away from the early Church 95% of what they did would stop. If the Holy Spirit is taken away from today's Church, 95% of what we do would continue."

## The Volatile Holy Spirit.

The Holy Spirit is wild, not in the sense of irresponsibility, but in the sense of unpredictability. He is as unpredictable as the wind, a metaphor of Him given to us by Jesus (John 3:8). Therefore we should be unpredictably the same – if we are being led by the Spirit.

**Summary.**

___

The Holy Spirit is lovely. He is personal, full of comfort, strength, wisdom, care, compassion, and is perfect in all His counselling, teaching, love and kindness. The enormous advantage of living beyond the cross and resurrection of Jesus (as we do), is that His Holy Spirit has been made available to every human being on earth. Thus everyone can know Jesus personally, can relate to Him, can be redeemed by Him, and can live with Him for ever. How? The Holy Spirit only and always promotes Jesus. They are inseparable. He has exactly the same characteristics of wise and kind perfection that Jesus has, and is so humble that He hides behind His Lord and Friend.

And then teaches us how to do the same.

# The Upper Room Discourse.

Mandy Gilbart-Smith is a good friend of mine and one of the best Bible teachers I have yet to meet. She lives in Comberton, Cambridge. She said that one of the first things that Jesus said in the Upper Room Discourse (John chapters 13-17) was *"A new command I give you: love one another. As I have loved you, so you must love one another. By this everyone will know that you are my disciples, if you love one another.'"* (13:34-35). Then He answered all the disciples' questions, starting with Peter's "Lord, where are you going?" and, at the end in 15:12, He says again *"My command is this: love each other as I have loved you."* That was the beginning and the end of the things that He wanted them to know. I think we Christians need to take that to heart.

But in the bits in between Jesus said some other very important things, and this is neither the time nor the place for me to go through them all. So I want to highlight the things He said about the Holy Spirit. Jesus was about to be crucified and leave the earth in a recognisable human form. He was to be replaced by the Holy Spirit and it was better that He leaves and the Spirit replaces Him (16:7) because the Holy Spirit would be everywhere where Jesus in His body couldn't be. The Holy Spirit would make Jesus present with everyone throughout the earth so that we could all know Him. So let us look at the things Jesus said the Holy Spirit would be and do.

*"And I will ask the Father, and he will give you another advocate to help you and be with you for ever – the Spirit of truth. The world cannot accept him, because it neither sees him nor knows him. But you know him, for he lives with you and will be in you."* (14:16-17).

1. He is an advocate. THE Advocate. A lawyer acting on our behalf. We cannot get a better or more competent advocate than the Holy Spirit.

2. He will be with us for ever. Every day, every moment, all our lives and beyond.

3. He is the Spirit of Truth. Jesus is the Truth. The Holy Spirit is the Truth and everything He will share with us is unvarnished, transparent Truth.

4. He will be invisible to the world - those outside of Jesus. Note the "cannot". That is an absolute. The world *cannot* know Him. That makes a Christian's perspective very different from the perspective of everyone else.

5. You (we) know Him. For the disciples the next sentence would be true – the Holy Spirit was *with* them and would be *in* them. They could

not have the Holy Spirit indwelling them yet, because Jesus had not yet been crucified so had not yet sent Him. We can. We are born again of the Holy Spirit, so that sentence does not apply to us. But it applies to the outsider and to us before we became Christians. The Holy Spirit is *with* them, drawing them to Jesus, and the moment they surrender to His sovereignty, the Holy Spirit comes *in*.

6. It is worth contemplating the enormity of the fact that the Holy Spirit can live *inside* us. That is God living inside us. Almighty God. Inside. United. The coming and work of Jesus was so utterly amazing and effective that it gave God the opportunity radically to change the whole of mankind – his past, his present and his future. Mankind can now live in a personal relationship with Almighty God in a friendship bond that is eternal and equal. What an utterly mind-blowing, eye-watering, knee-bending, open-mouth silencing scheme!

I think we need to take note of these things. How come intelligent people cannot seem to understand what we are trying to tell them? The answer is that there is a realm of knowledge and understanding (heavenly) that is impossible for any human being to understand. They need to be given the capacity to understand, and that can only come by Revelation or infusion from the Holy Spirit. Educating people can never make anyone a Christian. Only the Holy Spirit can open people's eyes. We can win a battle but lose the war if we try to persuade people by argument. Prayer and listening vertically is the key – do what the Holy Spirit tells you to do and say. Otherwise shut up and listen; both vertically and horizontally.

*"But the Advocate, the Holy Spirit, whom the Father will send in my name, will teach you all things and will remind you of everything I have said to you."* (14:26).

1. The Holy Spirit will teach us. Actually, He is the only one who can. Every one of us is utterly ignorant of the things of God. Only the Holy Spirit can open our eyes to see and understand truths that belong exclusively in God.

2. But then, He will teach us *all things*. If only we could grasp even a small part of the utter sovereignty of God over absolutely everything, and retain it for our daily walk, we would get insights and initiatives into a thousand things that we should have no human right to know. The Holy Spirit puts us right on all things. For example, in our education

we are taught many things. But the Holy Spirit will give us God's perspective on all of them, and He will put right what is in error. I have pointed out elsewhere that man's perspectives on Politics, Economics and Religion are entirely false. The Holy Spirit will teach us true ways of doing things, transparent ways of thinking things, insightful ways of human behaviour, and correct ways of behaving. (We can, of course, decide not to take God's advice. But experience over the years will teach us that living with our own decisions always leads us into trouble).

3.  He will *remind* us of the things that Jesus has taught us. That is, all things. Not just scripture or past revelation. If we could only grasp the fact that He is prompting us all the time and if only we had a handle on how to hear Him and believe it is He who is speaking, our lives would be lived in sunshine and fruitfulness all the time. Besides, our memories fail. God does not have a memory; He IS and knows all things. But He also has placed us into time, and yesterday is easily forgotten, so He understands how we can lose a lesson of time past. Besides, Jesus has also lived in time.

4.  The Holy Spirit imparts the things of *Jesus* (John 16:14 later). There is no competition here. The Holy Spirit, Jesus and God are totally united in all things. They all speak with one mind. Be sure you know that.

*"When the Advocate comes, whom I will send to you from the Father – the Spirit of truth who goes out from the Father – he will testify about me."* (15:26).

No one can get any right perspective about Jesus unless the Holy Spirit reveals Him. C.S. Lewis has written a lovely essay entitled "What Are We To Make Of Jesus Christ?" It is well worth reading. We cannot dismiss Jesus; we either believe His extraordinary statements or regard him as an idiot – on the level of a man who calls himself a poached egg. He does not give us any room to regard Him as anything in between. He is not a moral teacher: He is King of Kings and Sovereign Lord Almighty.

So, if we want people to know about Jesus, we need to be filled with the Holy Spirit and ask Him to open the eyes of the blind we confront.

*"Unless I go away, the Advocate will not come to you; but if I go, I will send him to you."* (16:7).

1.  The NIV translates the Greek word *"paracletos"* as Advocate. Other translations use the word Counsellor, and some Comforter. It basically means "one called alongside to help." Each word has a different perspective, but they all apply to the work and place of the Holy Spirit.

2.  There was a definite order in God's visit to the earth. First came Jesus. Jesus then had to be crucified, raised and ascended to be glorified. (*"Up to that time the Spirit had not been given, since Jesus had not yet been glorified."* (John 7:39)) Then He could send the Holy Spirit. We have a record of the timing. Jesus was 40 days with the disciples after He had risen from the dead. Then He sent the Holy Spirit onto them on day 50 at Pentecost. In these discourses, Jesus says that both He and His Father would send the Holy Spirit. Thank you Lord; You did.

*"When he comes, he will prove the world to be in the wrong about sin and righteousness and judgment: about sin, because people do not believe in me; about righteousness, because I am going to the Father, where you can see me no longer; and about judgment, because the prince of this world now stands condemned."* (16:7-11).

I heard a superb Bible study on this from Pope John Paul II in Perú back in 1982. Even the highly critical Peruvian Evangelicals were surprised and blessed.

1.  So what is the world's perspective on sin, righteousness and judgement? How are they wrong? Jesus' answers are not immediately clear nor humanly logical. But let us take what He says and consider each in turn.

2.  Sin. The world is wrong because everything they consider concerning sin – ignoring it, rebuking it, punishing it, avoiding its consequences etc – is the wrong way to tackle it. Jesus has dealt with it. It is forgiven; not a worldly consideration. But I wonder if you saw the underlying aspect of Jesus' statement? THE fundamental sin is not believing in Him. That is what the Holy Spirit reveals to each individual.

3.  Righteousness. I am far from convinced that I have full revelation on this one, but this is what the Holy Spirit has so far come up with. The world's view of righteousness is based on Law. No one can obey the Law. But the world is as if it is shut within a cave and unable to see righteousness from God's perspective. Therefore they make more and more laws then strive to obey them and fail. They live in guilt, fear

and effort striving after something which is unobtainable. The only righteous Man who has ever lived has gone back into heaven, so they are blind to the fact that righteousness is a gift from Jesus, and they can see Him no more. It is the Holy Spirit's job to *convict* them of missing righteousness altogether.

4. Judgement. It is satan who brings guilt and condemnation because of sin and lawlessness. It is as if he makes mankind feel guilty because he himself is condemned, and knows it. (I often wonder why satan and his angels have no capacity or even ability for repentance).

5. These three – sin, righteousness and judgement – are interconnected. They are the three things that destroy people's peace and contentment. God has made mankind to live in peace, to love and be loved. But these three forbid that, and the world's ability to deal with them is, simply, wrong. It is the Holy Spirit's task to *convict* the world of their errors in the way they handle them. The world's ways simply don't work. We can see that in the UK and Europe. More and more Laws are being written until no one is free to do anything without breaking at least one of them.

*"But when he, the Spirit of truth, comes, he will guide you into all the truth. He will not speak on his own; he will speak only what he hears, and he will tell you what is yet to come. He will glorify me because it is from me that he will receive what he will make known to you. All that belongs to the Father is mine. That is why I said the Spirit will receive from me what he will make known to you.'"* (16:13-15).

Whenever there is repetition in scripture (as here), there is a reason for it. Mainly emphasis. This is *exactly* what God wants us to know about the Holy Spirit. Notice that last sentence: Jesus gives the Holy Spirit the things He wants Him to say and do. That is one of the ways that the Trinity is united.

Read John 13 – 17 – the Upper Room Discourse. Jesus said some beautiful things in those chapters that all of us should soak ourselves in. We all struggle through life's difficulties. But these chapters will bring us back into faith in Jesus the One True God and the One True Man.

# Ministry.

Threading the Holy Spirit opened my eyes to something I had never seen before. It came in a daily Bible verse given to me: *"He has made us competent as ministers of a new covenant—not of the letter but of the Spirit; for the letter kills, but the Spirit gives life."* (2 Cor 3:6).

Before, I had always taken this personally. It was one reason why I have written so much against the Law and against legalism. "The letter kills" represents legalism. "The Spirit gives life" represents God's new way with mankind.

God gave Law to highlight our sin, because Law is absolute and perfect. As we compare ourselves with the righteousness that is given by Law, we know that we fail. Law's standards never change – they are always perfect. No human life can ever compare with Law's perfection. That is why "The letter kills".

Law is of earth. There are no Laws in heaven. That is the way by which the things of the Spirit overcome and exceed the things of earth infinitely. The ways of the Spirit (especially the Holy Spirit) are utterly different from the things and ways of earth. As the heavens are high above the earth, so the ways of the Spirit exceed the things of earth (see Isaiah 55:9).

I have noticed that many Christians – those who should be living wholly in the Spirit and by the Holy Spirit – live by the letter of the Law. I am not just referring to the secular Laws of the nations in which they live, but the Laws of the Bible, by the rules laid out in the Bible. They read their Bibles and, with their minds, wills and determination, they obey what is written. That, in my understanding of the scripture above, is sin. The reason is simple – it is all of man and not of God.

God's way is that we should only live by His inputs, His suggestions, His grace, His ways. That would make a life a living thing, relying on the living inputs of the Holy Spirit, rather than the dead words from their Bibles. Many Christians will object to my analysis. They tell me that their Bibles are living treatises, and verses jump out at them as they read it. That "jumping out" is, indeed, the work of the Holy Spirit. But the work of the Holy Spirit is always a "now" word. To be choosing to live by what we remember from our previous reading of the Bible is to live by works, not by grace. We should not live by the Law but by grace (Rom 6:14) – even by the Laws of scripture.

Of course, and to clear it up, working on earth only with our talents, intelligences, skills and efforts is always dead. What we have done may be nice and helpful, but it is a product of time. Therefore nice but dead. Only what is done by the Spirit is eternal and living in a way that God would understand and require it.

All that is by way of introduction.

If we walk by the Spirit, we all have a ministry from God. What I had previously seen from that verse was that *I* had a ministry; what I now have insight on is that *we all* have a ministry from God. Regardless of how unintelligent we might or might not be, doing what the Holy Spirit asks of us brings God's Life wherever we are and in whatever we are doing. *All* living by the Spirit brings Life.

If we are still living by our obedience to Bible regulations, we stifle the work of God within us. The letter kills. Even if we are overcoming our vulnerabilities by human effort and self-control, we are inhibiting or stopping the work of the Holy Spirit within us. The Spirit brings life, and life in all its abundance. The Spirit enables us to overcome our difficulties and limitations. The Spirit gives us life – He is living. It is part of the New Covenant that Jesus established on our behalf. That is what the verse at the top says. The Spirit gives to each of us a *ministry*.

By ministry, Paul is talking about bringing Divine Life to bear on the present situation we are involved with. Jesus has promised to lead us every moment of every day, and He has a unique and chosen pathway that we each tread. On that pathway Jesus wants us to minister *life*. In doing that, we live far above a normal human existence. We bring supernatural life to bear on every moment of every day. Paul is warning us to stop living by the Bible, and start living by the Spirit.

"Ministry" here is not what we would normally classify as ministry – like preaching, pastoring, or leadership. It is simply ministering Jesus' *Life*.

I am fully aware that the Holy Spirit inspired the whole Bible (2 Tim 3:16). But those words from yesterday only have life if they are, *today* and *now*, given life by the same Holy Spirit. Not from our own brains, but from Jesus through His Holy Spirit. So, as we walk, we seek God's inputs all the time. They may indeed come in the form of a scripture highlighted by the Spirit in a moment of time (they did with Jesus in His temptation in the desert); they may also be a story recalled by Him; they may be a word of knowledge; they may be words articulated our own unique way to the person we are talking to; but they must be by the Spirit and in the Spirit if we are going to walk with Jesus.

The scripture at the top reminds us to live right and not wrong. Jesus Himself put it this way: *"Do not work for food that spoils, but for food that endures to eternal life, which the Son of Man will give you. For on him God the Father has placed his seal of approval."* (John 6:27). Only in Jesus is there Life. All else is death. Even the letter of the Bible kills.

But for all Christians, the Holy Spirit has opened a way to have an eternal Ministry of Life. Grab it.

# A Guide, a Comforter Bequeathed.

From Wikipedia. "Harriet Auber, 1829. Harriet was sitting in her bedroom one day, looking out of the window, meditating on a sermon she had heard that morning, when an idea for a hymn poem came to her. Not having pen or paper nearby, she took off her diamond ring and etched the verses on the window. The hymn was there for many years afterward, but unfortunately, the pane was cut out and stolen after her death. Ironically, the subject of the hymn is the inner working of the Holy Spirit, a work that is largely invisible, though we can see its outward effects. An ethereal message scratched on glass seems a fitting emblem for Him."

I beg you, read these verses carefully, slowly, prayerfully, and absorb their truth into your innermost soul. May their truth all become a part of you for ever.

*Our blest Redeemer, ere He breathed*
*His tender last farewell,*
*A guide, a comforter, bequeathed*
*With us to dwell.*

*He came in semblance of a dove,*
*With sheltering wings outspread,*
*The holy balm of peace and love*
*On earth to shed.*

*He came in tongues of living flame*
*To teach, convince, subdue,*
*All powerful as the wind He came*
*As viewless too.*

*He came sweet influence to impart,*
*A gracious, willing guest,*
*While He can find one humble heart*
*Wherein to rest.*

*And His that gentle voice we hear,*
*Soft as the breath of even,*
*That checks each fault, that calms each fear,*
*And speaks of Heav'n.*

*And every virtue we possess,*
*And every conquest won,*
*And every thought of holiness,*
*Are His alone.*

*Spirit of purity and grace,*
*Our weakness, pitying, see:*
*O make our hearts Thy dwelling place*
*And worthier Thee.*

It is good to know that the occasional sermon that a preacher preaches results is a reminder such as this one that lasts for all of time. What the Vicar preached in those days blesses us still by being applied through this hymn. Humm it inside you all day long.

# Rationale for the Holy Spirit.

It is my personal opinion that the most astonishing thing that Jesus accomplished on the cross was to enable God to send His Holy Spirit down onto all mankind. Why do I think that?

Before Jesus came, the Holy Spirit was given a very limited access to individuals. Only a few experienced His presence. That was because their lives were still sinful, and God cannot live with anyone who is still self-determining – God's will and man's will are mutually irreconcilable. So the Holy Spirit was only sent to a very few special people for special occasions.

But now the Holy Spirit has been sent right across the earth. He has access to everyone because all the barriers which separate man from God have been dealt with by the one God-Man Jesus. The Holy Spirit is everywhere all at the same time. He sees all and knows all. He searches the deep things of God (1 Cor 2:10), so He knows the will of God for every individual.

Now see some other things that the release of the Holy Spirit implies.

With His presence in our hearts we have been brought right into the heart of the Godhead. Father, Son and Holy Spirit live within us. Jesus said, *"On that day you will realise that I am in my Father, and you are in me, and I am in you."* (John 14:20). In other words, Christians have been integrated into the Godhead, and the presence of the Holy Spirit is not only the guarantee of our inheritance (Eph 1:13-14), and our position in Christ, but the confirmation that God and Christians are One. Jesus is the Head and the church is His Body (Eph 1:22-23). It is absolutely astonishing that humankind has been brought from the depths of degradation, rebellion and separation right up above all other creatures (including angels) and right into the Godhead itself. We are the Bride of Christ as well as the Body of Christ. We are seated with Christ in the heavenly realms at God's right hand (Eph 2:6). *"God demonstrates his own love for us in this: While we were still sinners, Christ died for us."* (Rom 5:8).

See this also. God has begun to restore the whole earth to His original intention. He has dealt a mortal blow to the whole fabric of man-made institutions. The whole world system has been weighed in the balances and found wanting, its cultures and ways of living have been declared empty, useless and dead. They will all be replaced by God's system. God, who is in everything and through everything, runs this whole universe by the Trinity's own power and infinite ability, but by grace, kindness, wisdom and goodness. God also knows (and has told us in the Bible) that the vast majority of humankind will not accept the redemption and restoration that He has freely provided (Matt 7:13-14). Therefore they will press on in their self-centred ways and self-destruct the whole world.

So how is God going to restore His ways to the world?

He is choosing individuals, from among the people, who love Him back and will do His will. He brings them closer to Himself throughout their lifetime, and then removes them, preserving them for later. At the Second Coming of Jesus God will give to each of them a new resurrection body that is eternal. This body will be like Jesus' resurrection body and will be far better than Adam's original super body. These people will reign with Jesus over the earth for a thousand years, and then with Him over a new heaven and a new earth and over the whole universe on into the far distant future – as the Bride of Christ. God has seen that it is impossible for Christians to restore God's original intention for the earth while there are still self-determined people running it. So Jesus will deal with all of them when He returns in power and great glory. Only He can do it.

But do you see the future that God has in mind for us? He is going to sweep away this beautiful earth and cosmos and replace it with a more beautiful one over which the Bride of Christ will reign with Him for ever. So He has started small. He talks to individuals and reveals Himself to them so that they can choose Him instead of themselves. When they choose Jesus, he sends them the Holy Spirit to be their guide and guard for ever. Again and again the New Testament tells us that it is the Holy Spirit who is God within us, and is the key to knowing whether we have the real thing or just a human counterfeit.

Let's see what the Bible says about how the Holy Spirit works within us.

We are born into the spiritual family of God by the Spirit (John 3:6). We live by the Spirit (Rom 8:5). We walk in the Spirit (Gal 5:16). We pray in the Spirit (1 Cor 14:15). We speak in the Spirit (1 Cor 2:13). We worship in the Spirit (John 4:23-24). We sing in the Spirit (1 Cor 14:15). We have the mind of the Spirit (Rom 8:6). We are led by the Spirit, *for all who are led by the Spirit are sons of God"* (Rom 8:14). The Spirit guides us (John 16:13). The Spirit is our strength (Acts 1:8). He is the Spirit of wisdom (Eph 1:17), the Spirit of truth (John 16:13), the Spirit of revelation (Eph 1:17). Through the Spirit we overcome fleshly desires (Gal 5:16). We cast out demon spirits by the Spirit of God (Matt 12:28). The Spirit helps us in our weaknesses (Rom 8:26). We have access into God by the Spirit (Eph 2:18). We are being renewed in the spirit of our minds (Rom 12:2). God has not given us a spirit of fear, but of love, power and self-control (2 Tim 1:7). The Spirit sanctifies us (makes us more holy) (2 Thess 2:13). If we live by the Spirit we are delivered from the supervision (and bondage) of man's law (Gal 3:25). We develop the fruit of the Spirit in our natures (love, joy, peace, patience, kindness, goodness, faithfulness, gentleness and self-control) (Gal 5:22-23). The Spirit is the guarantee of our inheritance (Eph 1:13-14). He is exactly like Jesus (John 16:13-15), who will never abandon or forsake us (Matt 28:20, John 14:18). The Spirit has power (Acts 1:8). The Spirit talks to us (1 Cor 2:11-12). He is the Spirit of holiness (Rom 1:4). The Spirit cleans us up (2 Cor 7:1). He is the Spirit of meekness and humility (Phil 2:1-4). There are also supernatural gifts from the Holy Spirit that enhance our ministries (1 Cor 12:7-11).

At the same time, the Holy Spirit brings Jesus into our hearts. Jesus is our Shepherd, our Guide, our Guard, and the Alpha and Omega – the whole purpose of living, the beginning, the middle and the end of all things for us. He is our Husband, our friend, our lover and our greatest prize. If we have got Jesus, we've got everything. If we don't have Jesus, we've got nothing. The Holy Spirit is both the sign and seal inside us (Eph 1:14) that all things are ours through Jesus, for ever (1 Cor 3:21-23). Jesus is the eternal Yes (2 Cor 1:18-20), the answer to every prayer, every perception and every dream of goodness. All things are possible in Jesus (Matt 19:26, Mark 10:27). The works that He did on earth are also ours to do, and even greater works than His because He has gone to the Father (John 14:12).

The Christian culture is utterly different from the perceptions, the attitudes, the systems and the very fabric of the world in which we live, because it was designed and is being arranged by God Himself. This world and all that is in it is passing away. But the Kingdom of God is growing and lasts for ever (Is 9:6-7).

*"For to us a child is born, to us a son is given, and the government will be on his shoulders. And he will be called Wonderful Counsellor, Mighty God, Everlasting Father, Prince of Peace. Of the increase of his government and peace there will be no end. He will reign on David's throne and over his kingdom, establishing and upholding it with justice and righteousness from that time on and forever. The zeal of the LORD ALMIGHTY will accomplish this."* (Is 9:6-7).

# Handling Prophecy.

Just how much of modern prophecy should we receive? I come to this question with a lot of caution and trepidation. But let us go back into history and try to trace prophecy in general (rather than specific) as we read it.

The Old Testament is full of prophecies. In those days there was little writing. And what was written seldom lasted long because of the fragility of papyrus. There were many prophets in Israel in those days who spoke God's words to the people in prophetic form, and there is little record left of what they said. They were people for their particular generation, not for ours.

Others prophesied and wrote their prophecies down. Those which came from God were collected and collated and we now have them in our Bibles. We only have the written prophecies – we no longer have any of the verbal ones.

When you, like me, read the Old Testament prophets, you will probably find that there are many things in them that seem to be irrelevant to us today. There are prophecies about Moab, Egypt, Amon and other surrounding nations that may or may not be relevant. Have they been fulfilled already? Is there a double fulfilment? How do we know? How can we tell?

The answer to that difficulty is, in fact, simple. We ask Jesus to tell us. But that leads us to another difficulty. Jesus, being God, is full of wisdom. There are prophecies and words in scripture that are hidden from us. They are hidden in meaning, hidden in fulfilment, and hidden in their ability to multiply. (That is, many scriptures have double, treble or more interpretations, and some are only personally applied by the Lord to individuals rather than to the wider body of Christ). God is complicated and unpredictable, and much, much bigger than any of us earthlings can see or know.

Thus, interpretation of prophecies is more of a subjective matter than a universal matter. There are exceptions to that, which I will deal with below. Whether a particular prophecy is relevant to me and my nation or situation is entirely up to the Lord to reveal it to me. If He does not speak to me, then that prophecy is irrelevant to me.

Still dealing with scriptural prophecies, here a New Testament statement is relevant: *"Above all, you must understand that no prophecy of Scripture came about by the prophet's own interpretation of things. For prophecy never had its origin in the human will, but prophets, though human, spoke from God as they were carried along by the Holy Spirit."* (2 Peter 1:20-21). That applies to Biblical prophecies. We can assume from that that all Biblical prophecies have been sieved by the Lord, so that the human element has been removed or minimised from them. That there is a human element involved is clear from the Apostle Peter's description above.

Paul also told us *"Do not quench the Spirit. Do not treat prophecies with contempt, but test them all; hold on to what is good, reject every kind of evil."* (Thess 5:19-22). This tells us many things. It tells us to live, walk and think by the Holy Spirit – so, do not quench Him. It tells us that we can despise prophecies, and dismiss them out of hand. It tells us to test them all. It also tells us that prophecies can contain that which is good and that which is evil (that is, of man). Conclusion? Beware. Prophecies must be treated with caution and wisdom.

Paul and Peter were both New Testament Apostles. According to God's ways of doing things, they therefore must be seriously heeded. But they were also living in an age in which there was little writing, and much preaching. What they *said* is rarely recorded for us. We only have what they wrote. We trust the Holy Spirit entirely that what has been written down for the whole Christian Church in the Bible is directly from God. What they *said* was only relevant to their day and generation.

It is worth my pointing out that that is no different to what we have today. Last Sunday's sermons are, in their whole, forgotten. What is remembered from them is what the Holy Spirit injected into the hearts and minds of the listeners at the time. And that will, 100%, be different from everyone else. The purpose of a sermon is to change today's Christians with the eternal communication of Jesus. We remember only what He has said to us from the sermon or from the prophecy. All else is irrelevant and can be discarded – even if we don't remember much of it.

Ian Andrews, a reliable Christian prophet and healer, said that on a good day 70% of prophecy was from God, and 30% was from man. On a bad day, the reverse applied. It is impossible to eliminate the injections of the prophet himself or herself from a prophetic word. Every preacher preaches uniquely, and every prophet prophesies uniquely also. That is, the human element is never absent from the word given. (It is the same with writings - like mine. I cannot avoid my own perspectives being injected into what I write). The human element includes the experience of the prophet, their theological background (always limited), their present walk with Jesus, what they have read recently, the state of the nation in which they live, their own meditation on the subject (again, always limited), and even their spiritual internal state at the time of prophesying. To find what *the Lord* is saying through the curtain or veil of human transmission, is the point.

I think that those prophecies that are fully confirmed as coming from the Lord are those written down in the Bible. Only. Modern prophecy *has* to be tested. Those prophecies nearest to Divine communication are those whose principles line up with Bible scriptures. Others are, I suspect, *subjectively* interpreted or received. What do I mean? I mean – are they for me? Do they apply to me and my situation? Do they apply to my immediate environment or local area? What proportion of them applies to my nation? Do I believe and receive modern-day prophecies anyway? What is my spiritual relationship with the prophet? Do I think, as some do, that the Lord runs the universal Church today like He did in the Old Testament days? Should we accept the validity of all modern prophecies without question? Does the opening line of "Thus says the Lord…" make it valid, whatever the rest of it says?

Personally, I think not. All prophecy, said the Apostle Paul, has to be tested. So, who does the testing? If I am walking with Jesus, then surely those prophecies that do not get His confirmation in my heart, do not apply to me or to my situation. If I am in leadership with others, then the Lord's confirmation has to be 100% between us all. One doubter is enough for the rest of us to hold back, because the Lord's will can *only* be confirmed in unity. It does not seem to me to matter if the prophet is well known, has excellent credentials, has a good track record and so on, every prophecy of his has to be tested among the local Christian group. Is prophecy a new wave of Divine activity? I doubt it, especially if it is taught to be "The Word" for today. If it clashes with scriptural principles, then it cannot be from the Lord.

Christians, beware. Christians, be wise. Christians, be cautious. Christians, "let the peace of God guide you in every decision you make" (Col 3:15). Jesus *must* be Lord of all. Not man. Do not despise prophecies, but do make sure we test them.

# Unconventional Jesus.

Everybody lives with conventions. Or, if you like, everyone lives conventionally. They are patterns of behaviour that people have inexpressively succumbed to, often without deliberate choice or even thinking about it. Those who live with conventions (all of us?) normally do not break them, but live in contentment under them. Breaking conventions often leads to trouble, and people generally want to live in peace.

So, for example, I was in a Church last night. Someone had laid out the chairs in straight lines, fairly wide apart. That Church, those chairs. At one stage someone came along and straightened one of the chairs because it had twisted. It had become conventional to keep it that way in that Church. At one point I got up and repositioned a chair for a little girl because her Mum had sat in hers. I broke the convention. No one said anything, of course. They liked it. But none of them would have done it themselves – breaking the conventional pattern.

Churches are full of conventions. Our non-conformist Church has a time of worship, followed by the notices (and birthdays), followed by a sermon, in which the kids go out for their age-adjusted ones. No doubt your church has a pattern of worship somewhat like that. Anglican and other Churches who run by liturgy, are predictably the same all over the world. I suppose it all helps to keep the church stable; those who change the pattern of worship every Sunday normally find that they bring insecurity to the congregation, unless "change" becomes the norm, when people might object when today's service is a copy of last Sundays', and routine arrives back, instead of change! Anyway, we are predictable sheep, and gladly fit into patterns of behaviour that do not cause disruption, and we call those patterns conventional.

The reason why I am writing things like this is that I have got to the place in my walk with Jesus when I try to do whatever He prompts me to do, and on time. That causes me to be unconventional – to do things which normal people wouldn't dream of doing, because they are hindered by conventions. My actions don't normally disrupt (although they sometimes do!), but they are unusual. Sometimes they cause eyebrows to rise. Some people shrug their shoulders and say to themselves, (and often to others) "That's just Dick. You can't really tie him down, or trust him to do the normal thing." Some people even think that I am doing it just for fun, or just to stir others up – that I am a deliberately disruptive person. Some have seriously accused me of doing that. I do not need to justify myself. But I do need to explain.

First, though, we need to look at Jesus. Someone read part of John 6 last night in Church. There Jesus said if anyone did not eat His flesh and drink His blood, they would have no life within them. Notice His audience. They were Pharisees and Jews, steeped in the Old Testament, where the drinking of blood in any form was strictly forbidden and disgusting to them. Now here He was telling them that they should be cannibals and vampires – of His own body and blood. So controversial was that that *"From that time many of His disciples turned back and no longer followed Him."* (John 6:66). They couldn't handle it or stomach it. Jesus later explained to His disciples, *"The words I have spoken to you are Spirit and they are life."* (6:63). In other words, it's a metaphor. But, even bearing in mind the Old Testament, Jesus was giving them new truth straight from heaven. When Jesus asked Peter if he also wanted to go away, he replied, *"Lord, to whom shall we go? You have the words of eternal Life."* (6:68). So, even though Peter might not have understood what Jesus was saying, he still followed on. John must have remembered, otherwise he would not have written it down.

Think through all the miracles that Jesus did. All of them broke the conventions of His time. Healing, raising from the dead, walking on water, healing on the sabbath, changing water into wine and so on. I know they were miracles, and we marvel at them all. But we also need to see that, after Jesus had been filled with the Holy Spirit, He broke every rule and norm of their society (having lived conventionally for 30 years beforehand).

Why was He doing that? Jesus was bringing back what God had wanted in the first place, and that Adam and Eve performed before they fell. Jesus and they only did what God wanted them to do, regardless of *every* other consideration. Adam and Eve had no other considerations. But we have made thousands. Some Jews might have thought that He was doing it just for controversy's sake, and some modern critics might have put it that He was "playing devil's advocate." But He wasn't at all. He was simply doing what God asked Him to do at every point in time.

I am increasingly finding the same. As I walk with Jesus and strive to do only what He wants me to do, I am breaking through conventions of many kinds. I only want to do His will, and it seems that few others want the same, and few others would even dream of doing the same. Few others seem to understand. They don't even seem to understand the way God works, what God wants and how God communicates those desires to us. How can I possibly give you an example? They are happening every day. Just walking God's earth brings His perspective on everything that I am doing, and He has an opinion on everything. More and more I am refusing to listen to the norms and conventions (even if I know any of them), and simply do what Jesus is asking. I think that He is so good and so wise in what He says and does, that my confidence in Him has grown enormously, and now outweighs every other consideration. He *has* to be right in everything He suggests. That is my experience, anyway. Therefore doing His will actually gets good things done for the majority of a day. Walking without Him is like walking through syrup or deep mud. By contrast, walking with Him is like walking through air.

Jesus broke the sabbath laws. Not deliberately to shock the Pharisees, as some might say. But His one and only priority was to do the Father's will, whatever the consequences. And it got Him into trouble (as it sometimes gets me). Indeed, it got Him killed. Silly Pharisees – fancy thinking that if you kill a person you don't like or who conflicts with you, that's the end of it. It certainly wasn't with Jesus – especially if the one you are fighting is pure goodness and truth. He came back from the dead and changed the world. God cannot be stopped. For instance, I have been stopped preaching in my church – for reasons I won't bore you with. But it has driven me underground to write these books. So the majesty of God cannot be hindered. It always finds more ways for goodness to prevail.

This I can assure you – Jesus will lead you into much trouble, especially as you commit yourself deeper and more regularly into His will for you on earth.

Enjoy His wonderful unconventional adventure!

# Foreground and Background.

**W**hen I do something, that is the foreground. That is what is gaining my attention at a moment in time. But it is based on a background. I make my decision to do something now based on what is going on in my life, what has been going on in my life, and what all my decades of experience have taught me. It's the background that causes me to react in a particular way in any given situation.

For all of us, our childhood home has had a great influence on us, and forms the background to our foreground (daily) actions. What our parents taught us, what their perceptions and manner of life were, those are the things that form the long-distance basis of our actions. So, a trivial example: my parents taught me to put my knife and fork together when I had finished eating a meal. They said it indicated to everyone else that I had finished. So I still do that at every meal.

Other experiences throughout our lives alter, add or modify our today's behaviour. The background accumulates. Hopefully, our consequent actions improve over the years. Most of our actions are instinctive, and we do things because we do them *this* way, barely thinking why we are doing them. For example, a nurse rushes to help a victim in an accident. Ten years earlier, the chances are that she would never have done that. But now that she has been trained in nursing and had experience of sicknesses and disasters, she now acts by involving herself in the accident. Her changing background has influenced her foreground.

Most of us do not remember our backgrounds. And in our foreground actions we do not pause to think "Now what should my reaction be to this situation, and why should I react that way?" We simply get on and do it (or refrain from doing it).

Then into our lives comes Jesus. Surrendering our lives to Him is often caused by some traumatic incident that caused us to turn His way. Whatever it was is immaterial and unique to us as an individual. But His presence in our hearts and lives has completely reorientated our whole being. From then on, His inputs increasingly govern our foreground actions. His healing of our internal negatives, for example, stop us reacting violently, with swearing, angrily, or just plain negatively. Instead, now knowing He disapproves of those kinds of reactions, we go for different ones He has cultivated in us – like patience, peace, prudence, forgiveness and positivity. Jesus' way of life has gradually reorientated our background, set it (or is setting it) on a very different foundation, and other people notice that we have changed, particularly in our early years. The background influences our foreground.

Now there are two remarkable things that also happen when Jesus comes into our hearts.

**First**, we gradually realise that Jesus has an encyclopaedic knowledge of the whole of our background – every second of it, from our conception until now. That could be scary, but it is not because He stamps the lot with His forgiveness. It really does not matter what He knows because He never condemns us for any of it. But He *knows* it. And, remarkably, He takes into account every bit of it when He asks us to do something.

So, He is always right in His suggestions for a thing that I can do, because He does not restrict His knowledge to a single now situation. He includes all my background in His thinking. Then, He *has to* incorporate perfect kindness as well, perfect gentleness, perfect justice, perfect knowledge of now, perfect knowledge of the future, perfect knowledge of all past, perfect eternal knowledge of the future and perfect knowledge of the Divine plan for the world and the cosmos. He also has a full handle on the lives of everyone else involved in my immediate situation, and He guides to fit in with them as well. All that is included in what He is suggesting I should do at this point in time. That is why, when He asks us to do something, we *can* actually do it. Regardless of our Now agenda, He knows and we know that we can drop that immediately, and do what He is suggesting immediately. That is what Jesus did on earth when other people interrupted Him.

If we think about it, Jesus' guidance is far, far better than any guidance we had before we became Christians. How we acted before was based on our limited, shallow, narrow, individual experiences of life. (Which is why we went wrong so often). But now, Jesus' guidance is absolutely full of everything we have no knowledge of and no control over whatsoever. *His* way is complete and perfect. Our way was always one-dimensional and pathetic.

**Second**, God has wonderfully given us a Bible. In it is a sieved record of what God has been up to on earth from the very beginning. "Sieved" because it would be impossible for Him to include everything He has done in one volume. What remains is everything everyone on earth ought to know to get the best handle on who God is, what He does and how He does it. That therefore enables anyone on earth to form an intimate relationship with Him, because "God is love." (1 John 4:8).

The Bible is also a behaviour manual. It not only tells us what God can do for us in our lives, but it tells us how to do it. Let me quote one such passage: *"Therefore, as God's chosen people, holy and dearly loved, clothe yourselves with compassion, kindness, humility, gentleness and patience. Bear with each other and forgive one another if any of you has a grievance against someone. Forgive as the Lord forgave you. And over all these virtues put on love, which binds them all together in perfect unity. Let the peace of Christ rule in your hearts, since as members of one body you were called to peace. And be thankful."* (Col 3:12-15).

Those of us who are committed to Jesus love our Bibles. We read it avidly, know it intimately and follow it conscientiously. We feel a real stimulus as we read it, especially in our early years as a Christian. It is worth my pointing out that that stimulus was the Holy Spirit talking to us. There are many who worship their Bibles because through it they have found peace and encouragement. But quietly, humbly and prudently, the Holy Spirit is the One who is speaking. The Bible says that: *"...the letter kills, but the Spirit gives life."* (2 Cor 3:6). Without the Holy Spirit's life-giving inputs, the Bible is a dead book.

So now we must be careful. There are two ways of living that I have noticed Christians regularly follow. The first is to follow the Bible's teaching, with the Holy Spirit in the background gently steering them where to go and, through it, what to do. The second is for the Holy Spirit to do all the guiding in the foreground, with the Bible as back-up in the background. These two ways of life, summarised, are:

1.   Follow the Bible's ways and have the Holy Spirit gently steering in the background, or

2.   Follow the Holy Spirit directly, and have the Bible as the background back-up.

So, Christian, which of these two ways do you follow right now? Both seem legitimate, but one is obviously better than the other. Which is the Bible's recommended way? What is heaven's foreground/background method of living a Christian life, and what is man's way of living a Christian life? And what are you going to do about it?

# Think time.

12

Just pause for a moment. Give time to understand this quote from C.S. Lewis (from *Christian Reflections*). I had to read it a few times myself to get the full impact of what he was saying. You, cleverer and more learned than I, will probably get it immediately. Have a go:

> "*The good is uncreated; it never could have been otherwise; it has no shadow of contingency; it lies, as Plato said, on the other side of existence. It is the **Rita** of the Hindus by which the gods themselves are divine, the **Tao** of the Chinese from which all realities proceed. But we, favoured beyond the wisest pagans, know what lies beyond existence, what admits no contingency, what lends divinity to all else, what is the ground of all existence, is not simply a law but also a begetting love, a love begotten, and the love which, being between these two, is also imminent in all those who are caught up to share the unity of their self-cause life. God is not merely good, but goodness; goodness is not merely divine, but God.*"

At the heart of the universe, and the spiritual world beyond this physical universe, is goodness. Goodness precedes all things, surrounds all things, encapsulates all things, drives all things, and is intrinsically intertwined within all things. God did not create goodness. God is goodness. If we can assume that the God who has revealed Himself through our Bibles, and, particularly, in Jesus, is the very same God who precedes all things, creates all things, founds all things, fulfils all things, completes all things, and is, in the end, all things, then what we have found by knowing Him is without price. We are "favoured beyond the wisest pagans."

We who know Jesus have, miraculously and without any knowledge, capability, effort or ability on our part, been discovered by the Being who is beyond all things. He is the root cause of all things. We have come straight to the Head of all existence. There is nothing outside of Him, nothing beyond Him. He is the beginning of all things, the designer of all things, the constructor of all things, the maintainer of all things, the centre of all things, the end of all things. But in Him there is no end of anything except of wickedness. He does not finish, He completes. There is no concept of finishing anything with Him. He does not create without completing each created thing. Nothing comes to an end. Nothing created is unsuccessful. Everything outside of Him is, in the end, a nothing.

From Him is goodness. That is because *in* Him is goodness. Goodness permeates everything, is the root and branch of all things, and is the way that all things will travel, and the end to which they travel. It is not possible for goodness to be thwarted in any way, or at any time. Goodness is the centre of all creation, just because goodness is one of the central characteristics of this Cause of all things whom we name God. It is absolutely impossible for anything which He touches to be anything but good or anything but perfect. It cannot be otherwise. He cannot be otherwise. We, poor little earthlings, have to climb to the tops of the highest mountains to understand all this, much less absorb it into our beings as a lifestyle. One day we will realise that goodness cannot be avoided, cannot be thwarted, cannot be defeated and cannot be ended. This amazing and beyond-all-understanding God will make all things like Himself, good in every part and good in every way. Mr Lewis says, "Goodness is uncreated." It just IS. There is a level of Goodness that is beyond all human understanding. But that is the level which God is determined to restructure within us. He is going to recreate within us the same unmeasurable level of Goodness that exists without end in the Trinity.

But C.S. Lewis then mixes goodness with love. Goodness is not a touchy-feely thing. But love is. Goodness is a life. Love is a heart. Goodness governs. Love endears. Goodness directs. Love enables. The end of all things is goodness. The way to that end is Love.

It is astonishing to see the root attitudes of this amazing God manifesting themselves in human beings. Genesis (1:26) tells us *"Then God said, 'Let us make mankind in our image, in our likeness...'"* So what I have written above, when we have thought about it a bit, we will know to be true. We may not have thought about it before, no doubt. But at the root of every human life is the desire to be good, and the longing to be loved. That is because we are all made in God's image. That image has been seriously tarnished, as we would all acknowledge. But deep inside there remains remnants of who we intrinsically are and reflections of the enormous God who made us in His image. You may have noticed in the quote from Genesis above, that God is an "Us". *"Let us make man in our image."* Jesus tells us that that "Us" included Him. So does our Bibles. For example, Colossians 1:15-17 and beyond, says, *"The Son is the image of the invisible God, the firstborn over all creation. For in him all things were created: things in heaven and on earth, visible and invisible, whether thrones or powers or rulers or authorities; all things have been created through him and for him. He is before all things, and in him all things hold together."* The humble Jesus of the Gospels was, indeed, the God who created all things. That is why He says that He is the way to finding His Father. The best way. The only way. Jesus does all things well. In fact, perfectly. Jesus Himself is pure, unvarnished, untarnished goodness. Read the record and see for yourself. Even when He graced this dirty earth. And the reason He came is not because of His goodness, but because of His love. God has clobbered us – with goodness and love. Doesn't your whole body tingle with excitement at the very thought of it?

Only Jesus can recreate and complete in us the absolute goodness of which God is, and carry us there by the Love that resides for ever in the heart of the Trinity.

*Holy* Spirit.

13

I wonder if you picked up that little paragraph in the Prologue that gave the definition of Holiness? If you missed it, here it is again: The real root of the English word Holy is "Separate", or "Set apart".

I doubt if many of you readers thought that it meant that. It is probable that your concept of holiness in a person is of someone who has a beatific smile on their face, a look of infinity in their eyes, are almost completely disconnected with earthen reality, and have the outline of a dinner plate hovering above their heads. If so, you have probably been influenced by medieval artists trying to portray some religious saint or other.

By way of example, the vessels in the tabernacle (the tent of meeting) that God initiated through Moses in the wilderness, were designated "holy". There was nothing other-worldly about that. They were "set apart" exclusively for the purpose of the priests in the tabernacle, and were transferred to the Temple when Israel eventually became permanent in the Promised Land. They were never used for anything else. Solomon built the first Temple, and the vessels were placed in it. When the Babylonians under Nebuchadnezzar raided Israel, they captured the vessels (all made of silver and gold) and stored them in Babylon. *"While (King) Belshazzar was drinking his wine, he gave orders to bring in the gold and silver goblets that Nebuchadnezzar his father had taken from the temple in Jerusalem, so that the king and his nobles, his wives and his concubines might drink from them."* (Dan 5:2). *"Suddenly the fingers of a human hand appeared and wrote on the plaster of the wall, near the lampstand in the royal palace. The king watched the hand as it wrote. His face turned pale and he was so frightened that his legs became weak and his knees were knocking."* (Dan 5:5-6). The Queen introduced Daniel, who interpreted the writing. *"**Mene**: God has numbered the days of your reign and brought it to an end. **Tekel**: You have been weighed on the scales and found wanting. **Peres**: Your kingdom is divided and given to the Medes and Persians."* That night Belshazzar was slain, and Darius the Mede became King.

The Temple vessels had been "set apart" exclusively for God's purposes, and the misuse of them brought terrible repercussions to those who abused them.

Now let us examine what we mean by calling God's Spirit "Holy".

First, let us go, if I could put it this way, upwards. What does it mean in the Trinity? It means that God's Spirit, by calling Him "Holy", is "set apart" exclusively for God alone. That is, the Holy Spirit's nature is to honour, support, promote, exalt and worship God the Father and God the Son exclusively.

Of course, there is a logic in that. God the Father and God the Son are infinite in every aspect of their characters and natures. There is no lack of anything, and they stand above all the rest of existence to an infinite degree. They are infinitely wise, infinitely powerful, infinitely kind, infinitely humble, infinitely gracious, infinitely forgiving and … I am sure you can see the picture. The Holy Spirit is also infinite in everything, like the other Two, but the one characteristic that He has above all else is that He is "set apart" to belong to God exclusively, and to prefer God exclusively. He is infinitely powerful to proclaim and promote God only. That is His prime consideration.

Secondly, then, let us go downwards.

The work of the Holy Spirit on earth (or, for that matter, in the heavenlies) is exclusively to promote God. I think that God the Father is so humble and so unselfish that it is imperative that He has Another who will promote Him adequately, because He cannot promote Himself. It will be the same with Jesus. It will be the same with the Holy Spirit. None of them can promote themselves. The Holy Spirit will never promote Himself, but He will powerfully promote the Father and the Son. Exclusively.

When we look at Christian revivals over the centuries, we see that. We see the advent of the Holy Spirit coming down from heaven, Jesus being promoted as the Saviour of the world, and mankind falling face downwards in front of Him in humility and worship. That is what the Holy Spirit is continually doing by nature, and in that way He brings His own heart and His own desire to bear on mankind. We therefore come to worship Jesus just like the Holy Spirit does. And, I think, the Holy Spirit stays as long as Jesus is being promoted. If Christians turn from the worship of Jesus to worshipping the Holy Spirit instead, He disappears. He is "Holy," if you get the implications of the real nature of that word.

So let me try to work out, very roughly, what happens to us in our daily walk with God.

Jesus is the Human Being. He is the one who lived on earth perfectly. Therefore He is the one who can steer any human being, in their unique lives on earth, in a perfect manner. Thus Jesus said about the Holy Spirit in John 16:14, *"He will glorify me because it is from me that he will receive what he will make known to you."* So the Holy Spirit will promote Jesus, and Jesus will tell us what to do to live a perfect life on earth.

For example, Jesus prompts me to go down the town to the bank to put in some money that has just come in. As I walk down the street, I start to worship the Lord, sing a Christian song, or pray, often in tongues. That will have been prompted by the Holy Spirit – generating worship to the other two Members of the Trinity. A kind of "That's right. He's the greatest. Worship Him. He's got the whole world in His hands. Go for it, young man. Listen to what Jesus says, and do it, because He's always right." While the Holy Spirit is promoting what Jesus is asking us to do, He is robustly promoting Jesus. He cannot help but do so.

So, now let me try to deal with some other activities of the Holy Spirit.

**Repentance.** In order to become a Christian, we have to repent of our birth lifestyle. It is the Holy Spirit who prompts that in us. Why? Because He is telling us to turn away from our lifestyle and turn to Jesus, who, in the Holy Spirit's opinion, is the greatest human being in existence, and can help us to change our lives to be approved by God the Father. First, He tells us, we must die to this world and all it offers. Then He tells us to confess our sins. That is repentance. It is the beginning of our being "set apart" towards God.

**Rebirth.** To become a Christian, we, having first of all repented, need to be born from above into God's family. The Bible is clear that we are "born of the Spirit" (John 3:6). So, the Holy Spirit produced the seed that became Jesus. *""How will this be," Mary asked the angel, "since I am a virgin?" The angel answered, "The Holy Spirit will come on you, and the power of the Most High will overshadow you. So the holy one to be born will be called the Son of God."* (Luke 1:34-35). It was divine seed, but made human by being incorporated into Mary's human egg. So the Holy Spirit also produces the seed for our divine rebirth. That makes every Christian a kind of "clone" of Jesus. We have the same divine seed as Jesus had, appropriately modified to our uniqueness. (It is a parallel to human birth. We are all "clones" of Adam, the seed that generated us from our fathers being appropriately modified to produce our uniqueness).

The Holy Spirit took Divine seed and made it human through Mary. Now the Holy Spirit takes divine seed and makes humans like Jesus.

Why is it that Christians start to abandon the things of earth, and start to focus their lives more and more exclusively towards God and His things? Why? Because that is the nature of the Holy Spirit, and therefore the nature of the seed that birthed us into God's family.

**The Filling of the Spirit.** When we are baptised in the Spirit, and are filled for the first time with Him, that zips us to the end of exclusivity. We stop compromising with the world, the flesh and the devil. We become flat out for God and Jesus. We become like the Holy Spirit – set apart exclusively for God.

And, of course, over time we leak. That is why we need to *"be being filled with the Holy Spirit."* (Eph 5:18). The Holy Spirit has only one thing in mind, and only one activity to promote – it is the total love for God and a total commitment to that love. He makes us like Himself.

I think here that I need to issue a warning. Becoming a Christian demands totality of everything. Everything earthly we might cling on to must totally go. Everything of heaven must totally grow. It is the very nature of the Holy Spirit, who births us into God, that there is no alternative to exclusivity. That is why our Bibles encourage us to be set apart exclusively for God. *"But as He who called you is holy, you also be holy in all your conduct, because it is written, "Be holy, for I am holy."* (1 Peter I :15-16). Let me retranslate that: "But as He who called you is separate, you also be separate in all your conduct, because it is written, "Be set apart, just like I am set apart.""

# Walking in Sin and Sun.

I start with sin. When Jesus said that He would never leave us or forsake us, that obviously included when we are sinning.

All of us will, no doubt, find that difficult. But stay with me. The normal human reaction to sin in others is to walk away from them. We do not want to be part of that sin, so we estrange ourselves both from the sin and from the person who is doing it. So, when everyone else is getting drunk, we choose not to be part of it. We walk out. Or we walk away. Or, if we cannot do either, we stay there tight lipped but smiling, say nothing, and do not participate. In the same way, we expect Jesus to do the same.

There is reasonable Old Testament justification for that. It says somewhere that God is too holy to look on sin. "(I found it – Habakkuk 1:13)."

But how can Jesus do both – not to look on sin and to stay with us always? He cannot deny Himself, so His promise never to leave us or forsake us means that when we are sinning, He is still with us, and somehow is looking on the sin. That would be hard for us to understand, so let me give you an example from my experience that might give some glimpse into how He does both at the same time. The illustration is driving a vehicle, say car.

Those of us who do that (and the principle applies to everything we do on earth because we are under Law doing everything) will drive their car beyond the official speed limit. Please don't deny it – every driver does it. Even one mph. Technically we are sinning – breaking the Law.

We do it accidentally many times, but let's take the case that we are doing it deliberately. We are in a hurry, and so we speed. We argue with ourselves that our behaviour is justified, but with the Christian we will be (should be) discussing it with the Lord. If we are not, then we are refusing to talk to the Lord about it, and that is a greater sin. We so often think that when we are sinning the Lord would automatically disapprove, so we don't talk to Him about it when we are deliberately breaking the law. How can we expect the Lord to protect us and guide us if we are not in "communication mode"?

So, we discuss the reasons with Jesus. Now I have found that He does not do what I would expect Him to do, or what another human being would invariably do. (The human being would not entertain any excuse, he would just say "Slow down.") But Jesus is not a normal human being. He would listen to our argument carefully. Many times He would not argue against what we are doing; He remains impassively with us, discussing it without emotion, and often without comment. If He is not obviously disapproving of it (He doesn't always), He allows us to continue in His peace. He knows that if we get caught by the police for speeding, then we carry the consequences; He doesn't. It's our responsibility to drive within the legal limits and prudently, but *we* hold the responsibility for driving every way we do. He will still warn us to slow down if there is danger ahead that we cannot see (He always does that), and He has not abandoned us when we are doing something bad. He is with us, helping us, but not commenting unless there is something that He wants to say. That is how He manages to live with the sin and not abandon us. He does it by refraining to comment.

The first point I want to make is that we need to be sharing our whole life experiences with Jesus. The second is that He wants us to. He wants to be driving cars along with us. After all, He has allowed that kind of technology to happen in His good earth, and He goes everywhere that any technology travels, and with anyone who is accessing both it and Him together. He neither approves nor disapproves (and He certainly never condemns because we are living in the age of grace); His eternal will is to walk with us, stay with us and never leave us any moment of every day of our lives. That is God's perfect will for every born again Christian – indeed, for all of mankind. Jesus is reliving His life on earth through each one of us. Perfectly. And, in His view, for us to live perfectly is always and only to do the will of God. He is interested and involved in every minor decision that we make, and is frequently prompting us with tiny details. "Sit there, not here." "Why not clean your teeth now?" "You've forgotten your glasses." "You left your pills in the bathroom."

But when we are speeding are we not breaking the Law? Certainly. But that law, however sensible it is, is a law made by man and not by God. I recall Jesus saying that to the Pharisees when they accused Him of breaking the law, which He was clearly doing at the time (indeed many times). (See Mark 7:6-8).

So *the only law that prevails in all things* is to do the will of God all the time. That is, walk with Him and find out His will on every occasion, whatever we are doing. That is how to live a perfect life – even when we are deliberately breaking man's laws for reasons which we are in the process of discussing with Him. It is far better to be talking with the Lord and listening to Him than either to ignore Him or to walk by Law and not by Grace (Rom 6). If indeed He sees the reason why we are driving beyond the designated speed limits, He will still remain in communication contact with us, and not express disapproval. That is, it is *my* responsibility to drive according to man's laws, it is *His* responsibility to stay with me, talk with me, save me from hidden dangers and warn me of impending trouble on the road. By not saying anything against my breaking the Law does *not* mean that He is approving of my doing it. *Silence does not mean either approval or disapproval.* He will make sure that, my having made the decision to drive beyond the speed limit for reasons that I have talked with Him about, I will get to my destination on time and safely. Which, so far in my long life, He has nearly always enabled me to do.

If there is a hindrance stopping me doing what I am planning to do, then I take that to mean that the Lord does not want me to go that way and He has a better way for me to go. If there is no room on the ferry, then He has a better alternative. I don't need to get frustrated; I remain in His peace and seek His perspective on the next step.

I find that walking with the Lord (walking in the Holy Spirit, or with Jesus) is infinitely variable on a daily basis. Everything changes. All my plans form a distant and general idea of what might happen today, but the details are far from predictable. The Lord changes everything to fit into a bigger agenda – His. So, when the ferry is full and I have to travel another way, I find a bus has broken down and I can fill my van with many stranded passengers – a thing that I could never have anticipated or planned. In the end, all my plans are fulfilled, but none of them in the way that I had planned for them to be fulfilled.

As I have contemplated the life of Jesus, I see that that is exactly what happened to Him throughout His ministry years. All sorts of things stopped Him on His way. He dealt with each in peace, accepting that the change in plan came from the Lord. Jairus is a good example. Jesus said that He would go to Jairus' house to heal his daughter. On the way the woman touched the hem of His garment and He stopped to heal her and assure her of her faith. Meanwhile, messengers came to tell Jairus and Jesus that it was too late – the girl had died. But Jesus took no notice. If the Father had said that He should go and heal the girl, He would go and heal the girl. Nothing would hinder that happening. What is "too late" from a human perspective is never too late for the Lord.

The reason why this happened to Him and happens to us is that we are limited geographically to one body in one space and time, but God is not. He is omnipresent and omniscient. So when He sees something that needs to be done by a willing slave of His, the willing slave will be permanently ignorant of it, until the Lord prompts him. Just do it as it flares up in front of us. Don't get angry, frustrated or difficult. Remain in peace, trusting the Lord. He is training us to be eternal.

Many times we have given up following the Lord's leading, thinking that the barriers that have erupted in the way are an indication from the Lord that it was never right in the first place. But I would maintain that every barrier will break down in front of the Lord's will. We just have to believe (as Jesus said to Jairus) and drive the barriers away in His name.

I think that these sorts of spontaneous things happened far less to Jesus before He was baptised and filled with the Holy Spirit. His life before that was listening to His Father, combatting temptation at all points, doing what He had to do as a man, and learning to follow Father. Nothing miraculous happened during those days. Of course. Nothing will happen to any of us if we have only been born again and not been filled with the Holy Spirit; just like Jesus. If we want to live a miraculous life, and do all sorts of things that are common to the Holy Spirit but very uncommon to human beings to do, then be filled with the Holy Spirit.

Matthew 4:4 says, *"Man shall not live on bread alone but on every (spoken) word that comes from the mouth of God."* Hear, listen, learn, speak, do. If we have not yet discovered how He speaks in our minds, how *can* we expect to do His will? So, walk in His sunshine.

Those who have not grasped the secret of listening to exactly how the Lord speaks in our minds and/or have not been filled with the Holy Spirit will never fully understand this chapter.

# The Transforming Model of Abraham.

Abram (High Father) had his name changed to Abraham (Father of Many Nations) when his heart was transformed by God. Here is the background:

Abram was born in Ur of the Chaldees, in what is now Iraq. He was the youngest of his family, born when his father Terah was 70. The family's religion was pagan, and they worshipped many gods. Terah was a maker of gods. If we work out the ages of all those ancestors, we will find that Abram was alive at the same time as Noah, although Noah apparently lived near Mount Ararat in Turkey, where the Ark finally rested. Abram was 60 years old when Noah died, and was almost certainly living in Harran by then – not far from Noah. Shem, Abram's ancestor, was also alive. All Adam's genealogy and the Creation and Flood stories would have been handed down to their descendants, and to Abram in particular.

God spoke to Abram when he was still in Ur. There is no record of Terah his father sharing the same faith. Terah and his family set out to go to Canaan, but he stopped and settled at Harran. Had he been called by God to go to Canaan? Harran was north of Israel in what is now southern Turkey, and is both a district and a town. The upper reaches of the River Euphrates are close by, and possibly Terah journeyed up the river from Ur on his travels. Terah died in Harran, aged 205.

That Abram should find and worship One God was a serious departure from the culture in which he was born. He swam against the flow. It must have been hard both for Abram as well as his family and friends to live together with such a discrepancy. It was so revolutionary, and Abram was so totally committed, that God Himself called Abram His friend. We, in our generation, can call God our friend, but for God to call Abram His friend was exceptional indeed.

Abram was freed by the death of his father. Soon afterwards God talked to Abram, and said, *"Go from your country, your people and your father's household to the land I will show you."* (Gen 12:1). God needed Abram to separate from his family, and sever from the whole of his background. Abram was now on his own, alone with God. God also gave him a promise with that call, and said, *"I will make you into a great nation, and I will bless you; I will make your name great, and you will be a blessing. I will bless those who bless you, and whoever curses you I will curse; and all peoples on earth will be blessed through you."* So, Abram and his wife Sarai and his nephew Lot and his family went south, not knowing where they were going. That, in itself, was an enormous step of faith (Heb 11:8).

God had to test His friend, and you can read of the traumas and adversities that confronted him from Genesis 12 onwards. Abram came through like gold, so God changed his name to Abraham – Father of Many Nations.

The thing that has stood out for me is that Abraham followed his God regardless of everyone else and everything else throughout his life. In Ur, in Harran and in Canaan Abraham followed God unswervingly. In his early years he must have had huge opposition from his father (maker of gods) and from all his contemporaries. When he was on his own in Canaan, loneliness and isolation did not deter him from remaining single-minded. When he had no heir, he believed God would be as good as His word and give Sarai a child at age 90, which He did. He even trusted God to raise Isaac, Abraham's child of promise, from the dead when he offered him as a sacrifice on the same hill that God offered His own Son Jesus 2000 years later (Heb 11:19). Abraham followed God single-mindedly, to the exclusion of all else. Which is why God made him the Father of Many Nations, as his name says. Paul, in Romans, picks out the phrase *"Abraham believed God and it was credited to him as righteousness."* (Rom 4:3, Gen 15:6).

I want to encourage you to follow Abraham's example. Every born-again Christian reading this will have opposition. You will be laughed at for believing in Jesus, and many of you will be persecuted. You may have your goods stolen, your house raided, your body tortured. You may even have to accept an early death and martyrdom, all your earthly dreams binned. Just how far are we prepared to go to follow our Friend Jesus?

Many Christians that I know have fallen away. They were strong in their youth, but the ravages of this world have defeated them, and far too many have suffered from what, in one sermon I preached many years ago, I called "The Barren Middle years". Jesus' parable of the Sower gives us some clues as to what can divert us off Him: trouble because of the Word, the worries of life, the deceitfulness of riches, and the lust of other things. We Christians have specifically designed opposition that God has programmed for each of us that is going to test our faith to the limit. As you read this, please ask yourself whether you are committed to Jesus for ever - *regardless* of what has happened, is happening, or may happen in your life.

I can leave you with a good key that will help your stickability: ONE DAY AT A TIME. Just today; just NOW. Am I committed wholly to Jesus NOW? You can ask yourself that same question every day of your life on earth. The rewards for sticking with Jesus are phenomenal.

How does that help? I cannot put it better than C.S. Lewis; "The Present is the point at which time touches eternity. Of the present moment, and of it only, humans have an experience analogous to the experience which God has of reality as a whole; in it alone freedom and actuality are offered them." (Modified from Screwtape Letters).

Abraham's model? Now, the present tense, is the only place where we and the Jesus of eternity can touch each other. That touch is the only way to remain faithful to Jesus during our walk through time.

# The Pattern of This World.

This morning my daily readings included this quote from C.S. Lewis:

*"There are three kinds of people in the world. The first class is of those who live simply for their own sake and pleasure, regarding Man and Nature as so much raw material to be cut up into whatever shape may serve them. In the second class are those who acknowledge some other claim upon them – the will of God, the categorical imperative, or the good of society – and honestly try to pursue their own interests no further than this claim will allow. They try to surrender to the higher claim as much as it demands, like men paying a tax, but hope, like other taxpayers, that what is left over will be enough for them to live on. Their life is divided, like a soldier's or a schoolboy's life, into time 'on parade' and 'off parade', 'in school' and 'out of school'. But the third class is of those who can say like St Paul that for them 'to live is Christ'. These people have got rid of the tiresome business of adjusting the rival claims of Self and God by the simple expedient of rejecting the claims of Self altogether. The old egoistic will has been turned round, reconditioned, and made into a new thing. The will of Christ no longer limits theirs; it is theirs. All their time, in belonging to Him, belongs also to them, for they are His." (Present Concerns).*

Compromise is the major behaviour of most Christians. They have one foot in this world and one foot in heaven. They are, like someone described to me when I was a young Christian, a "Mugwump", trying to live on both sides of the fence at the same time, with their mugs on one side and their wumps on the other.

They have picked up the thinking of the world, and stick to it. Maybe they thought the world's ways before they became Christians, and have continued to hold those views? Or maybe they have conversed with non-Christians, been unable to resolve their difficulties, and have therefore retained their unbiblical perspectives (and criticisms)?

Let me give some examples.

1. Who came before God? Or, who made God?

2. I can't see how a God of Love could have wiped out nations and peoples as He did in the Old Testament.

3. Surely nice people and good people have something of value in them for God to allow them into heaven?

4. Surely God will allow me a little flexibility to indulge my "innocent" craving(s) and/or lusts?

5. What about those who have never heard of Jesus? Do they go to hell too?

6. Scientifically, the Bible's view of creation, especially of its timing, must be rubbish.

7. "I bet Jesus scrumped apples from His neighbour's garden when He was a kid."

That kind of thinking is pure "world". It belongs to those who have heard about the Gospel and rejected it because those kinds of anomalies do not conform to their view of love or to their sense of justice. Their problem is that they have never read their Bible, never believed the whole truth contained in it, or don't really want to anyway. Why does God simply destroy people on what appears to us to be a whim? Or is He so selfish simply to banish everyone who does not love *Him?* If that is what God has revealed Himself as being, then I reject Him.

C.S. Lewis above has shrewdly observed the three categories of people – the non-Christian, the compromising Christian and the whole Christian.

So how can I resolve those kinds of difficulties, particularly for the Christian? First, God hates compromises. In Rev 3:15-16, on His view of the Church in Laodicea, God says, *"I know your deeds, that you are neither cold nor hot. I wish you were either one or the other! So, because you are lukewarm—neither hot nor cold—I am about to spit you out of my mouth."* I think the original Greek reads "vomit", rather than "spit" there. As I said, God hates compromises and compromisers.

Second, for those who compromise, there is a level of faith in God Himself and in His word through the Bible that is very shallow indeed. They maintain that their opinion is just a valid as God's, and when God's opinion disagrees with theirs, they reject God's, and stick to their own. Do they not know that

God designed and made this whole cosmos? Do they not know that God is *perfect* in everything He is and does? Can they not even see that their own bodies are miracles of construction? Can they not accept that God's *perspective* is also perfect and Sovereign in every respect, and, even though that perspective contrasts with their own, that He can be trusted in all things – even when they don't understand? It seems to me that anyone who disagrees with a perfect God seriously lacks the faith that He requires, and, in my experience, are heading straight for pain. God is able to allow satan to inflict pain on us to such an extent that we will have yet another thing we cannot understand and cannot cope with, forcing us to trust Him despite our blindness and ignorance. The book of Job is a salutary lesson for us all. Implicitly to trust in God, regardless of the pain, is a lesson we all need to know in full. How is it ever possible for any human being to understand the infinite? What bridges the gap is faith – a belief that God is never wrong, never evil, always perfect in attitude, word and action, and His love will extract the very best that is possible out of every situation and every human being. God will give to every person the very best that they deserve.

C.S. Lewis said in another place that in the end either we say to God "Thy will be done", or God says to us "Thy will be done." It is best to resolve that conflict as early as possible in life.

Members of the new Jesus' race must completely stop thinking the thoughts of Adam's race. They are wrong from every perspective. That is, compared with God's perspective. He said, *"My thoughts are not your thoughts, neither are your ways my ways,"* (Is 55:8-11). And 1 Cor 2:14 tells us that the world is *totally incapable* of understanding God's ways. See it: *"The person without the Spirit does not accept the things that come from the Spirit of God but considers them foolishness, and cannot understand them because they are discerned only through the Spirit."*

Therefore, Paul recommends this: *"Do not conform to the pattern of this world, but be transformed by the renewing of your mind. Then you will be able to test and approve what God's will is—his good, pleasing and perfect will."* (Rom 12:2). It is the *pattern* of this world, the way they think, (the way we used to think), thinking with the brain from the limited insights of this world only, that God tells us to get rid of for ever. To be filled with His Spirit, thinking His thoughts, eagerly following His suggestions only, doing His will, and giving as little time as we can to every way and idea from the world that tries to crush us – that is what a real Christian is. Renew your mind. Change the base from which your thinking originates. *"Set your mind on things above, not on earthly things. For you died, and your life is now hidden with Christ in God."* (Col 3:2-3). As C.S. Lewis points out above, "to live is Christ".

# God's Holy Spirit Strategy.

How did God plan to use the Holy Spirit throughout earth's history? I certainly do not have all the answers because the Lord has not written it in my Bible nor given me revelation, particularly about Old Testament times.

What I do know is that the Trinity is indivisible. So, the Holy Spirit came together with God the Father and Jesus the Son, wherever they came. But in differing and unconventional manifestations.

So, starting at the beginning, Gen 1:1 tells us that "In the beginning, God made the heavens and the earth." God the Father was there putting the creation together. God the Son was there, because He is the Word of God, so when the text says, "And God said…", that would be Jesus. And in verse 2, it says "The Spirit of God was hovering over the waters." The Trinity were all in agreement concerning the creation of earth and its environs.

I can only guess that God the Father held the presence of Jesus and the Holy Spirit in reserve until man had decided his future on earth. That is, whether Adam was going to obey God's single commandment not to eat the fruit of the tree of the Knowledge of Good and Evil or not. Once Adam had disobeyed and eaten it, God's redemption of mankind was established. It was then that God told Adam that he, Adam, would crush satan's head (Gen 3:15), and also be in trouble for the rest of his life and the lives of his descendants. That is the first reference to Jesus' role as a human being in the redemption plan.

The following 1800 years proved disastrous. There were no restraints on mankind, so all but a very few indulged prolifically in sin, to such an extent that God had to kill the whole of mankind in the global Flood, rescuing only eight in the Ark. God's ways were available for mankind, because the fruit of the Tree contained Good as well as evil, so mankind would still have God's inputs of Goodness going on in his mind. If only they had listened!

After the Flood, God imposed Law on mankind. Law was a behaviour device, governed by guilt, conscience and condemnation. Because Law was perfect in its demands for standards (rather than in its content, which would vary according to the nation in which it was written), the Holy Spirit's role was to bring conviction of sin into human hearts, thus restraining evil in the new generations. John 16:8 tells us that one of the tasks the Holy Spirit has is convicting people of sin. But then, does that only apply to New Testament times, or has His role been like that down through the ages? I do not know. What I do know is that mankind, since the Flood and the advent of Law, has suffered a guilty conscience throughout history. Conscience controls wickedness.

Then God had to introduce Israel to the world. It was through the narrow channel of Israel that God was going to introduce His Son to earth, so He had to plan Israel ahead. Hence the story of God's dealings with Abraham and Israel in the Old Testament. Even then, it was vital that Israel proved to be a failure in performing God's will. That would produce the Pharisees of Jesus' day, emphasising the huge contrast there would be between the way that God thought man should live on earth and the way that man thought man should live on earth. So important would that clash be that it was necessary for jealousy and rivalry to prevail over Jesus and cause Him to be nailed to a cross. God arranged that perfectly (Acts 2:23). Everything was prepared, even the birth of wicked men.

God's plan was to introduce Jesus at the perfect point in time on earth. God arranged for all things on earth (political, social, Jewish, Roman and the rest) to be in the right places for both the arrival of Jesus and the spread of the Gospel through Paul and the disciples afterwards. So, if it was necessary for Jesus to undergo crucifixion, then the Romans would have to be in charge of Israel, because crucifixion was a particularly Roman execution device. (Did you know that when the people of Israel were wandering through the desert to go to their Promised Land in about 1400BC, they camped in the shape of a cross? Work it out from the Book of Numbers).

Now one of the major things that God introduced by the birth of Jesus was that God, in the direct form of Jesus, would be enabled to live *inside* human beings. John 14:17-23 introduces that. Jesus inside. John 14:20 reads, *"On that day you will realise that I am in my Father, and you are in me, and I am in you."* In that same passage, Jesus spoke about the Holy Spirit coming to live inside: *"But you know him, for he lives with you and will be in you."* (John 14:17).

The change seems to be this: before Jesus came, God (all Three of Them) had access to people's minds. Probably only the mind. But now, because of the immensity of what the Cross achieved, God was prepared - all Three of Them – to indwell human beings. To live inside. That is the major reason why, when Jesus comes into a person's heart, they are filled with joy, reconciliation, forgiveness, grace and all the rest. The *light* includes the *life*. Those who put their trust in Jesus gain *eternal* life (John 3:16 and many other scriptures in John's Gospel).

There were occasions in the Old Testament when God sent the Holy Spirit *onto* certain individuals. This made them very bold to do God's will. That was emphasised particularly in the Book of Judges, with Othniel (3:10), Gideon (6:34), Jephthah (11:29), and Samson a number of times (13:25). Later the Holy Spirit came upon King Saul (1 Sam 10:10), and then King David, which is probably why the Psalms he wrote relate so powerfully with us today. But the gift of the Holy Spirit was restricted at that time to certain individuals and certain occasions – a kind of foretaste to what God had in mind after Jesus had been resurrected.

I have written elsewhere that the Cross of Jesus spans the whole history of earth. The redemption that it brings goes back to the beginning of time and travels to the end of time. That is because the Bible tells us of *"the Lamb who was slain from the creation of the world."* (Rev 13:8). I have no knowledge of how God applied that to those living before Jesus came to earth, celebrated by us on Christmas Day.

After the resurrection, Jesus fulfilled His promise to send the Holy Spirit down to all people, and that happened the first time at Pentecost. Now, the Holy Spirit has a number of tasks.

1.  He is *with* people before they become Christians, drawing them to Jesus (John 14:17).

2.  He comes *in* to people when they repent and give their lives to Jesus, and He comes in to their hearts and lives. The Holy Spirit makes Jesus known.

3.  He births people into God's family. (John 3).

4.  He comes *upon* people when they are filled with the Spirit. From then on they have heavenly power. Acts 1:8 is the promise of Jesus, *"But you will receive power when the Holy Spirit comes on you;"*

Now, in this Age of Grace, all three Members of the Trinity have come to live inside repentant human beings, empowering them to be transformed to be like Jesus, and giving them heavenly gifts and understanding which only a few in Old Testament times had.

The amazing thing is that God longs with all His heart that the Bride of

His Son Jesus should be numerically full, and belong inside His family. Instead of waiting until people on earth have died and assessed as to whether they might go to heaven or not, God has taken the initiative and invaded the earth, making heaven's beginnings available to every human being living on earth. Heaven is closer to each person than a brother, if only people would turn their hearts towards Jesus.

The dynamic work of the Holy Spirit, to beget us into God's family, to empower us, to transform us daily, to equip us to walk like Jesus did on earth, and to carry us in His arms into heaven when we die, is the role of God's wonderful Holy Spirit to us in this day of Grace. Father started it all. Jesus redeemed it all. Now the Holy Spirit completes it all. May the God of eternity be heaped and smothered with praise for ever!

# Giving Thanks.

18

I was walking down the street this afternoon when, from inside, a wonderful sense of joy and thanksgiving to Jesus welled up. It happens often. I praised the Lord and, indeed, gave Him thanks.

It then occurred to me that it was the Holy Spirit who generated that within me. It spontaneously came up inside me, and not because of anything that I had done to initiate it, although I was available for whatever the Lord wanted of me.

It then occurred to me that the Holy Spirit did not *do* it to me, as if giving me a gift. He was doing it Himself. That is, He Himself felt a great need at that moment to give Jesus thanks for who He is, and just did it. It was a direct communication between the Holy Spirit and Jesus, and was soaked in love and gratitude.

So how come I was caught up in it?

It then occurred to me that the Holy Spirit and I are one. Not one being, of course, but one. We are fused together inside. I am part of Him and He is part of me. So when He gives thanks in the Trinity, I sometimes get caught up in the celebration. It is quite spontaneous.

It was interesting to note that nothing of me was diminished in the incident. I lost nothing of who I was, who I am or what I do. I was (and am) still a unique individual, and my surrender to Jesus as my Saviour and Lord has in no way shrunk me from what or who I eternally am. God in no way destroys our individuality. He only enhances it. I am by far a better person by having the Trinity live inside me than I ever was, or could ever have made myself to be. Indeed, I am fully fulfilled and completed by that.

So what happened was that I was caught up in a smidgen of the praise of heaven. What is going on all the time in heaven, where the Trinity and angels are all fully submitted to one another in joy, worship, praise and thanksgiving to Jesus, I was in that instant a part of it. It was a bit like Elijah being separated from Elisha by the chariots of Israel in a moment of time and swept up into heaven in a whirlwind. (He stayed up there and I didn't. Yet).

I was part of heaven in that incident – and have often been there before. But what never occurred to me before was that I became part of the Holy Spirit's personal worship of Jesus. The miracle was that He was also part of mine.

Do you understand what that implies?

# Epilogue.

It is interesting that the number of chapters in this little booklet are fewer than in other booklets of mine. Why should this be?

Probably because the Holy Spirit is absolutely humble. He never pushes Himself forward. He is always hiding behind Jesus, honouring Him and promoting Him. The Holy Spirit is very difficult to nail down. Indeed, we cannot. He promotes the Father and the Son without reserve, and shies away from every form of self-exultation.

I lived through the Holy Spirit resurgence of the 1970's – 1980's. There, His hidden glory and power were restored, and He was greatly exalted once again. He had long been forgotten. The consequence of His being forgotten was that the Church had become powerless in both word and deed, and what remained were social human efforts. Like tea or coffee mornings. But His arrival and renewal gave power and incisiveness to preachers' words, new life to both conversations and activities, and many challenges to dull old Churches and dull old Christians. Miracles happened, and the gifts of the Spirit became normal. As did the teaching on the baptism and filling of the Holy Spirit, restoring the Biblical norm for the Christian Church. Heady days. Beautiful new life. Very humbling to dull old Christians like me, who thought they knew everything and, quite clearly, didn't.

But it was not long before He hid Himself again. Exalting the Holy Spirit does not last long. He pushes to the forefront the excellence of Jesus and the sovereignty of God the Father. The Holy Spirit is a true servant.

But the one thing above all others that I have found about Him is the freedom He brings. I am truly set free from all my sins and inadequacies, in that none of them are any longer a problem to me (or to Him). I have no heavy load on my back. And my daily walk is also free to do precisely what God asks me to do. In that walk God only asks me to do what is within my capability, within my availability, within my time, and within my delight. It is a pleasure and joy to walk "in the Spirit". That is the true freedom of living a Jesus Life here on earth. Even washing the dishes is a joy.

The greatest Servant of all, the Holy Spirit, teaches us all to serve like He does, and to promote everyone else above ourselves. Listen. Believe. Obey. Live. Rejoice. And dance (if your body lets you), all together with Him.

# About the author

Dick Bell was born in Kenya of a British family. His major love was aeroplanes, and, after his secondary schooling at Rossall in the UK, joined the RAF as a pilot. He became a Christian as a cadet at the RAF College Cranwell. He left the RAF after 20 years and became the main Bible Teacher at a Christian Conference Centre in Devon called Upcott, where he taught mainly children and teenagers for 26 years. He is married with one daughter and two grandsons. During his time at Upcott he took part in four Hovercraft expeditions on appropriate rivers across the world, under the leadership of Mike Cole OBE. Following the last expedition to Nicaragua, in 2000 he was called by God to take up full-time Missionary work there, where he founded the UK charity SIFT. His Missionary remit was four-fold – Initiate, Develop, Establish, Delegate. That enabled him to hand over the charity and begin a final new agricultural work on the Island of Ometepe in Nicaragua, where he also founded a new Church. He was prompted to write all the chapters in the Two-trees Series of books by the Holy Spirit since becoming a commuting Christian Missionary. He was granted an MBE in 2014 for his work in the Third World.

Printed in Great Britain
by Amazon